The SPIN®
Selling Fieldbook

Other Books by Neil Rackham

Major Account Sales Strategy

Spin® Selling

Getting Partnering Right: How Market Leaders Are Creating Long-Term Competitive Advantage (authored with L. Friedman and R. Ruff)

The SPIN® Selling Fieldbook

Practical Tools, Methods, Exercises, and Resources

Neil Rackham

Huthwaite, Inc.

McGraw-Hill

New York   San Francisco   Washington, D.C.   Auckland   Bogotá
Caracas   Lisbon   London   Madrid   Mexico City   Milan
Montreal   New Delhi   San Juan   Singapore
Sydney   Tokyo   Toronto

Library of Congress Cataloging-in-Publication Data

Rackham, Neil
    The SPIN® selling fieldbook : practical tools, methods, exercises,
and resources / Neil Rackham.
        p.   cm.
    Includes index.
    ISBN 0-07-052235-9 (pbk.)
    1. Selling—Handbooks, manuals, etc.   2. Sales promotion—
Handbooks, manuals, etc.   I. Title
HF5438.25.R343   1996
658.85—dc20   96-7902
                                                    CIP

18 19 20   FGRFGR   0 5 4 3

SPIN® is a registered trademark of Huthwaite, Inc. European SPIN® trademarks are held by Huthwaite, Ltd.

ISBN 0-07-052235-9

The sponsoring editor for this book was Betsy Brown, the editing supervisor was Fred Dahl, and the production supervisor was Donald F. Schmidt. It was set in Palatino by Inkwell Publishing Services.

Printed and bound by Quebecor

McGraw-Hill books are available at special quantity discounts to use as premiums and sales promotions, or for use in corporate training programs. For more information, please write to the Director of Special Sales, McGraw-Hill, Inc., 11 West 19th Street, New York, NY 10011. Or contact your local bookstore.

 This book is printed on recycled, acid-free paper containing a minimum of 50 percent recycled de-inked fiber.

Contents

7

Situation Questions

8

Problem Questions

11

Demonstrating Capability   *145*

12

Sharpening Your Skills   *167*

Introduction

The success of *SPIN® Selling* took me by surprise. While I was writing it, I had an uneasy feeling that the book might not be well accepted. And initial events made it seem that my unease would prove correct. My original publishers, who had persuaded me to write the book, cancelled the contract when they received the manuscript. "It conflicts with generally accepted sales ideas," they explained. Other publishers wouldn't touch it because they too thought it went against conventional sales wisdom.

Finally, McGraw-Hill agreed to publish the manuscript and *SPIN® Selling* became a best seller. Even more satisfying, it wasn't a flavor of the month book. Each year it has gained more new readers than the year before. The SPIN® model has become widely accepted in major corporations. In fact, half of the Fortune 100 companies use it to train their salespeople. Universities and business schools teach it, and the underlying research on the effectiveness of the SPIN® model has become a widely quoted case study in textbooks on evaluation methodology.

I say this not to brag but, oddly enough, to register a growing dissatisfaction. Although our work has influenced large and leading corporations, I'm constantly reminded that the majority of salespeople don't work for big organizations. Most salespeople, whether they sell products or services, work for small companies. My firm, Huthwaite, gets letters, phone calls, and e-mail every day from sole practitioners, individual professionals, and one- or two-person salesforces. These are people who have read *SPIN® Selling,* who are convinced that the ideas in it are right, but who now need further help and advice on how to put the concepts into practice. They don't have the resources or the numbers to justify attending Huthwaite's customized training programs, but they do need practical tools to help them take the next step.

I talked with many of these people—with an architect from New Mexico, a software developer from San Diego, a sawmill owner in West Virginia. I tried to be helpful and to answer questions but knew, as I put the phone down, that they needed more than just a few words of advice. Gradually the idea of *The SPIN® Fieldbook* evolved. It would consist of tools, exercises, and practical advice. It would help people struggling to turn good concepts into productive sales. It would particularly appeal to those in smaller organizations who didn't have access to our customized training programs. The only problem was finding the time to put it together.

My colleague Leni Gurin volunteered to search through thousands of pages of the books, articles, and programs I have written over the years and to cull from them useful material to help people sell better with the SPIN® model. With the addition of several new chapters, she has synthesized and expanded that material into a practical, step-by-step implementation guide. *The SPIN® Fieldbook* is the result.

Acknowledgments

Let me introduce Leni to you. Before Leni joined Huthwaite, she ran her own consulting practice for almost ten years, learning the hard way what it means to be an individual out there selling for a small company. She's also worked for large consulting practices, including two Big 6 accounting firms. Her practical experience in managing change and implementing performance improvement programs has given her a real sense of how to help people develop skills. She worked hard to communicate the ideas and suggestions in this *Fieldbook* in a way that would be useful and practical. If this book helps you, it's thanks to her efforts and down-to-earth approach.

Three others in Huthwaite deserve special mention for bringing this *Fieldbook* to pass. Sandy Rose and Pam Smith undertook the graphic design, and Elaine Lasky edited and proofed the manuscript. Elaine has worked with me for ten years, helping to prepare four of my books for publication. Sadly, she'll be leaving Huthwaite for a new career, and we'll miss her greatly.

The SPIN®
Selling Fieldbook

1

Using the *SPIN*® *Fieldbook*

Overview

I grew up in the jungles of Borneo in what's now Eastern Malaysia. My father was setting up schools in rural areas where education was unknown. I remember going up river with him to a newly opened country school to deliver notebooks for the students to write in. When we came back a month later, there, untouched on the teacher's table, were the notebooks we had left. The teacher explained to us, "These books are much too nice to spoil with children's scribbles. I shall wait until they grow up and leave school. Then I'll give them the notebooks." It sounded logical enough to an 8-year-old like me. Books weren't meant to be written in—or, if they were, they should be reserved for important and organized thoughts.

Why a *"Fieldbook"*?

Obviously, I'd never heard of a *Fieldbook* like the one you're reading now. This is not a book for leaving on the teacher's table until you have the skills. It's designed for you to use actively as you read it. That means it needs to be scribbled in. The words you read are, at best, 10 percent of the value from this book. It's what *you* write that counts. The *Fieldbook* is full of what we call "exercises." These are tools, tests, and frameworks to help you sell more successfully. Try them. *Really* try them. Just looking at the exercises will not help you sell better. However carefully you read each exercise, it's not until you write your responses that you begin to reap the value of this *Fieldbook*. Writing your answers to the *Fieldbook* exercises is important in two ways:

1. **Translation**

   Many of the exercises are designed to help you translate general concepts into the specifics of your own situation. From interviews with hundreds of the salespeople we've trained, clearly one of the hidden barriers that gets in the way of putting new selling ideas into action is this issue of translation. It's easy for smart salespeople to understand fundamental concepts, like the ones we describe in this fieldbook, on a purely intellectual level. The tough thing is seeing how these concepts actually work when it comes to selling your own products or services. The first step in putting the ideas you'll read here into action is to build a bridge between the concepts in this book and your own selling situation. That's what we mean by "translation." It's the process of taking general ideas and transforming them into specific actions that relate to your products and your customers. Translating concepts into tangible actions is an important step to improving your selling. Working through the exercises in this *Fieldbook* and writing down your answers will help you with the translation process.

2. Planning

A consistent finding about successful salespeople is that they put effort into planning. Ninety-nine percent perspiration and 1 percent inspiration is the way that Thomas Edison described genius, but he could equally have been talking about selling. The myth that great salespeople work by pure inspiration is just that—a myth unsupported by the evidence. Good selling depends on good planning more than any other single factor. Because of that we've included dozens of planning exercises throughout the *Fieldbook.* Even if it sometimes feels repetitive, work through these planning exercises. Remember that effective planning takes you more than half way to effective execution. Think of these planning exercises as a dry run for real selling. We can't be out on calls with you. We can't help you once you are face-to-face with that important client or customer. But we can help you to plan. Many of the significant improvements in selling that have been attributed to the SPIN® model have come from better and more systematic planning.

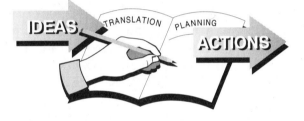

The SPIN® Model

You should ask two sets of questions before you invest time in anything—including this *Fieldbook*—that claims to help you sell better. The questions are:

What will this teach me?

What ideas, concepts, frameworks, or models are being recommended? How do I know these will work in my kind of sale?

How will this teach me?

What *methods* are used to communicate the idea or models?
Are these methods practical and realistic enough to help me sell better ideas?

We've started to answer the second question already. This *Fieldbook* is designed as a series of practical exercises to help you translate the ideas into plans for action. We've taken an approach based on actual experience helping thousands of salespeople, and so the methods here have been reality-tested. But how about the first question: *what* will this teach you? What are the underlying ideas that we're communicating? Where do they come from? How do you know that they will work? The underlying theory of successful selling that we're teaching in this book is based on something called the SPIN® model.

You'll read more about this model in the next chapter. In case you haven't met the SPIN® model before, here is a brief introduction:

- It's a set of ideas about how to sell successfully in large or complex sales.
- It's based on the most extensive research ever carried out about effective selling.
- More than half the Fortune 100 use it to train their sales forces.
- You'll find it described in detail in the best seller *SPIN® Selling* (Rackham, McGraw-Hill, 1988).

Getting the Most from This Fieldbook

As we've said, this is a book of exercises. So you'll get the most from what you write, not from what you read. If you follow the advice we give here, complete the exercises, and put them into practice in your own selling, there's a high probability that you'll get a measurable improvement in your sales. We say this based on the experience of the first thousand salespeople we trained to use the SPIN® skills. When their results were compared with a matched control group of untrained people, they showed an average increase in sales volume of 17 percent.

Will you get a 17 percent improvement? Unfortunately, that's an unanswerable question. It's like saying that a group of a thousand people lost an average of 17 pounds by going on an exercise and diet program. It shows that the program brings results, but it doesn't necessarily mean that you would automatically lose 17 pounds if you went on the same diet. How well such a program would work for you would depend on your present weight, your present dietary and exercise habits, your determination, and even your genetic makeup. You might lose 30 pounds or you might even gain some. The same is true of using these exercises to improve your selling. Your improvement will depend on your present level of selling skills, how adaptable you are to changing your selling habits, and—above all—on your willingness to learn. And, like diet and exercise programs, it will also depend on whether you adopt a systematic and sensible strategy for change. We know, for example, that the crash dieter who starves will almost certainly be less successful than the person who takes things at a slower pace and loses weight gradually. Exactly the same is true when it comes to changing your selling habits. If you try to read this book in a single day and then apply all its lessons in your next sales call, you'll be just like the crash dieter. You'll have tried to change too fast and you'll probably fail.

So, if you shouldn't take this book like a crash diet, how should you use it in order to get the most value? Here are four suggestions:

1. More Haste, Less Speed

Take it at a moderate pace. A *Fieldbook* shouldn't be like a novel that you can't put down because you want to know how the story turned out. We can tell you the punch line right now. It's this: by systematically working through these exercises, you can improve your selling. You don't have to speed through to the end of the book to get the message. Instead, once you've read the introductory chapters that give you an overview of the SPIN® model, slow down. Read one chapter at a sitting. Complete the exercises, try the ideas. Don't hurry through the book.

2. Stick to the Fundamentals

Like most instructional books, this one gets more complex as it goes on. The early chapters may seem basic. It's easy to dismiss these basic skills as elementary and to skip to the more exciting material later in the book. If you do this, you'll be shortchanging yourself. The early chapters are not elementary; they are fundamental scales. And that's very different. High performers everywhere, whether in sports, the arts, or selling continue practicing the fundamentals. A professional golfer doesn't stop working on basic putting, a master pianist still practices scales, and top salespeople continue to work at honing their fundamental selling skills. Believe me—I've worked with many of the world's top salespeople and I know.

I first had this lesson taught to me twenty years ago when I had the opportunity to go through a sales training class with a group of top performers from Xerox. At one point in the class there was an opportunity for participants to choose any skill they wanted to practice further. I'd seen less tenured Xerox people go through the same class, and they usually chose to practice one of the "advanced" skills taught on the program, such as price negotiation. So I was surprised that most of the top performers instead chose "basic" skills, like questioning. I wouldn't be surprised now that I've worked with so many world-class salespeople. They don't neglect the fundamentals and neither should you.

3. Alternate Theory with Practice

When you've finished a chapter and tried its exercises, spend a few days putting the concepts into practice in some real sales calls. The book *SPIN*® *Selling* contains a chapter "Turning Theory into Practice." Among the advice it offers is that nothing feels natural the first time you try it. Consequently, you should try any new idea that could help your selling at least three times before you decide whether it is working. So we would recommend that, after reading a chapter, you try out its ideas several times before going on to the next chapter. In that way, you'll give these ideas the best chance to add real value to your selling. Alternating each new chapter with plenty of tryout opportunities is a smart learning strategy.

4. Repractice Your Weak Spots

As you work through the book you'll find some areas that seem very natural to you and others that give you difficulty. Keep coming back to the difficult areas. If you find any area tough, leave it alone for a few weeks and then revisit it. Often these tough areas are where people with sufficient persistence make breakthroughs that dramatically change their sales results. There's an element of "no pain, no gain" at work here. The harder it is to develop a skill, the more valuable it may turn out to be.

The purpose of this *Fieldbook* is to help you learn and apply the SPIN® concepts and skills, both in your office and out "in the field." Our intent is for you to be able to *use* the *Fieldbook* exercises, tools, and the plans you develop—out there where they matter, on actual sales calls with your clients and customers. But enough introduction. This is a practical book and we haven't yet met a single exercise. We'll set that right in the chapters that follow.

2

Instant SPIN® Model

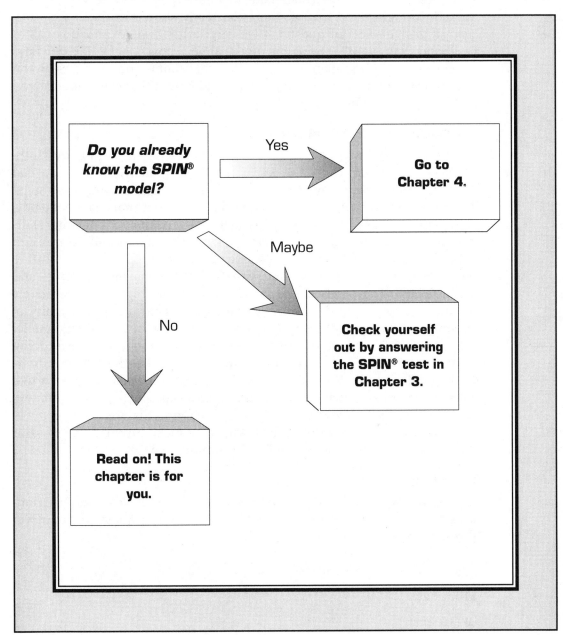

About This Chapter

This chapter is designed to give you an instant basic understanding of the SPIN® model. It isn't meant as a substitute for the excellent and informative book, *SPIN® Selling* (Rackham, McGraw-Hill, 1988.) If you haven't looked through *SPIN® Selling*, then you really should do so. It's a quick read, it answers lots of questions we can't address here, and it is full of cases and examples that bring the model alive. Above all, if you're the kind of person who is impatient with unsupported claims and promises, if you search instead for substance and proof, then you'll find the evidence you need in *SPIN® Selling*.

The Origin of the SPIN® Model

The SPIN® model was developed from a massive research study by Huthwaite of 35,000 sales calls. The research set out to answer a question that had been troubling many people in high-end business-to-business sales. Their question was this: Are there special skills that make someone successful in large sales? Or is selling just selling, so that the fundamental skills are the same whether the sale is large or small? Companies like Xerox and IBM, who sponsored Huthwaite's research, were preparing for a future where they anticipated that selling was about to become more complex and sophisticated. They had started to recruit and train high-end salespeople for this new world of the complex sale. They were finding that many of those recruits who had been outstandingly successful in making smaller sales, failed miserably in the new large sale environment. What was going wrong? Huthwaite's job was to find out. We traveled with many hundreds of their salespeople. We used a newly developed, objective research tool called behavior analysis to measure the skills of salespeople and to find out what the most effective ones were doing. We found that top salespeople in large sales did have a set of special skills. The most important set of skills that these successful performers had in common we called SPIN® skills.

Basic Findings

Before we get to the SPIN® skills themselves, let's look at some basic findings from this massive research study. The simplest question to answer through research was this:

In successful sales calls who does most of the talking?

❏ *The buyer?*

❏ *The seller?*

By counting the number of things said by each person in thousands of sales calls, we were able to confirm something that effective salespeople have suspected for a long time. In successful sales calls it's the *buyer* who does most of the talking. How do you get a buyer to talk? By asking questions. So it was no surprise to the research team to find that the most successful salespeople were those who asked the most questions. But not just any questions. It soon became clear that successful salespeople asked smart questions and they tended to ask them in a particular sequence.

Test Yourself

Write down four or five examples of questions that you typically ask during a sales call.

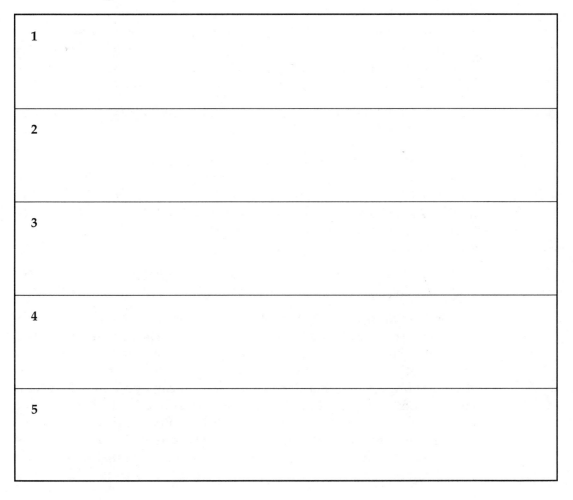

1

2

3

4

5

Now categorize your sample questions into two types:

1. **Factual questions about the buyer's present way of operating, e.g.:**

   How many people are there in this location?
   What turnaround time are you getting?
   How do you measure quality?

2. **Questions about problems, difficulties, or dissatisfactions or about the buyer's desire to solve these problems, e.g.:**

   Are you worried about competitive responses?
   What effect would that problem have on output?
   Are you looking for a faster process that would overcome this bottleneck?

Situation Questions

Questions of the first kind—that ask about facts or explore the buyer's present situation—are called Situation Questions. They are necessary questions. You can't sell without them. But look at your own examples and ask yourself this:

> *Who benefits more from these Situation Questions? Do I benefit more or does the buyer?*

Most people ask Situation Questions to obtain information that will give them the facts they need to sell. Take our examples, *"How many people are there in this location?"* or *"What turnaround time are you getting?"* This information may be very helpful for the seller but it doesn't do much for the buyer. Situation Questions generally benefit the seller. That's why our research showed:

- The more Situation Questions in a call, the less likely it was to succeed.
- Most people asked a lot more Situation Questions than they realized.

Successful salespeople ask Situation Questions, but they ask them economically. They do their homework. They find basic factual information from other sources, not from the buyer. There's a widely held belief in selling that's at least a century old. It suggests that buyers love talking about themselves and their businesses; so you can't go wrong by asking your customers to talk about themselves. If this belief is true, then you'd imagine that Situation Questions, which are often used to collect facts about buyers and their businesses, would be positively related to success. Unfortunately, this belief is pure myth. While it's true that most buyers would rather talk about themselves or their businesses than listen to a boring product pitch, research shows that the more senior the buyer, the less they like answering factual questions. As one purchasing vice-president told us, "When a salesperson wants to take up my time with discussion about hobbies, or wants me to teach them basic facts about our business, I get irritated. In today's world I'm too busy for that. I don't get much value from educating salespeople. Too often they ask questions that don't respect my time."

So, although you must ask Situation Questions, ask them economically. Make every factual question count. Buyers don't get a thrill out of telling you the details of their existing situation. Do your homework. Collect factual information from other sources and from more junior people.

Situation Questions at a Glance

Situation Questions	**DEFINITION:**	Finding out facts about the buyer's existing situation.
	EXAMPLES:	*How many people do you employ at this location?*
		Could you tell me how the system is configured?
	IMPACT:	Least powerful of the SPIN® questions. Negative relationship to success. Most people ask too many.
	ADVICE:	Eliminate unnecessary Situation Questions by doing your homework in advance.

Problem Questions

So, unfortunately our research team found that the more Situation Questions you ask, the less successful the sales call is likely to be. We say "unfortunately" because Situation Questions are the most frequently used of all sales questions, and they are the easiest of all questions to ask. But the good news is that the research found three other types of questions that are much more powerful than Situation Questions and are strongly related to success. In other words, the more that any of these three types of questions are asked in sales calls, the more likely that those calls will succeed. The first of these types we call Problem Questions. Problem Questions are about the problems, difficulties, and dissatisfactions that the buyer is experiencing with the present situation and that you can solve with your products and services. Typical examples are questions such as,

> *How satisfied are you with your present system?*
>
> *What prevents you from achieving that objective?*
>
> *What problems are you experiencing in this area?*

Inexperienced salespeople ask fewer Problem Questions than their more experienced colleagues. In fact, during the research we were able to predict quite accurately how long people had been selling by the number of Problem Questions they asked. Those with the most experience tended to ask more Problem Questions and to ask them sooner in the discussion. People new to selling, in contrast, tended to ask mostly Situation Questions and, if they asked Problem Questions at all, they asked them very late in the conversation.

Why is the level of Problem Questions higher in successful calls? Why is it so powerful to ask buyers about their problems? Think about it for a moment. The answer is that products and services—from cosmetics to computers—all sell because they solve problems for buyers. A good definition of a product or service is that it is a solution to someone's problem. Even products that at first sight don't seem to solve problems actually do so if you look more closely. Try these examples of products that are not obvious problem solvers and see if you can identify a problem that each of them solves for a potential buyer.

Product or Service	Problems It Solves for a Buyer
A Rolls-Royce	
A video game	
A tie with a picture of Elvis on it	

At first sight, none of these products seems to solve a real problem. What does a Rolls-Royce do that a Chevy can't? Both get you from point A to point B. The Rolls sounds like pure ostentation and vanity. And, of course, it is. And that's the problem it solves. It lets owners show status, it bolsters the sagging egos of the successful but insecure. And there are plenty of customers lining up to pay their quarter of a million who will testify to how severe the ego problems are that a Rolls can help to solve. How about a video game? It solves problems of boredom. And an Elvis tie lets the wearer solve the problem of how to look different, how to tell the world that the king still lives, or how to start a conversation. Although none of these is a "useful" business problem, they are problems none the less and the sales of Elvis ties, video games, and Rolls-Royces show that the problems they solve are very real for some people.

Think of one of your own products or services in problem-solving terms. Try to think of at least five problems it solves. And look for less obvious problems because they are often the ones that will make or break sales.

One of Your Products or Services	At Least FIVE Problems It Solves for a Buyer

Problem Questions are the raw material out of which sales are made. In later chapters you'll meet many exercises and activities to help you to plan and practice asking Problem Questions.

Problem Questions at a Glance

<table>
<tr><td rowspan="5">Problem Questions</td><td>DEFINITION:</td><td>Asking about problems, difficulties or dissatisfactions that the buyer is experiencing with the existing situation.</td></tr>
<tr><td>EXAMPLES:</td><td>What makes this operation difficult?

Which parts of the system create errors?</td></tr>
<tr><td>IMPACT:</td><td>More powerful than Situation Questions. People ask more Problem Questions as they become more experienced at selling.</td></tr>
<tr><td>ADVICE:</td><td>Think of your products or services in terms of the problems they solve for buyers—not in terms of the details or characteristics that your products possess.</td></tr>
</table>

Implication Questions

As we've said, experience alone is enough to teach salespeople how important it is to ask about problems. If you've been selling for several years, the chances are that you already have learned about the value of Problem Questions. If you are relatively new to selling—or if you are someone who only sells occasionally—then practicing Problem Questions is probably the single most important thing that you can do to improve your selling. However, the next type of question is one that doesn't get better with experience, and a lot of the most experienced salespeople we studied had a serious gap in their questioning skills in this area. In our research we found that skill in using the most powerful of all questions—what we call Implication Questions— doesn't automatically improve as you become more experienced. Top salespeople use a lot of these Implication Questions, but thousands of experienced but less successful sellers that we studied didn't ask these questions at all.

Before we look at Implication Questions in detail, let's start with a curious finding from the SPIN® research. Top salespeople, we found, tended to introduce solutions, products, or services very late in the discussion. In contrast, their less successful colleagues couldn't wait to begin talking about what they could offer. This finding held true across many industries. It was particularly pronounced in high technology, where salespeople often had exciting and innovative products they wanted to talk about. It was also pronounced in consulting and service sales, where consultants often felt they weren't providing value unless they were talking about solutions and approaches. What's so wrong about introducing products or solutions early in the discussion? Or, to put it another way, what's so right about waiting until late in the discussion before talking about what you can offer?

Let's examine the link between introducing solutions and sales success. Imagine you are a brand new salesperson.

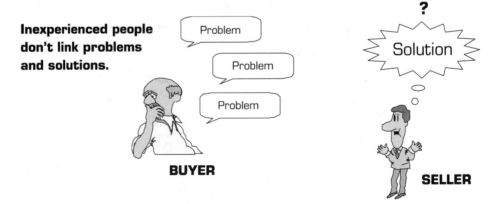

New salespeople, because of inexperience, may not see a clear link between a buyer's problems and the solutions they can offer. As a result, they may be reluctant to offer solutions. However, as salespeople become more confident, as they understand how their products solve problems, and as they ask buyers more about problems, the link between problems and solutions becomes much clearer in their minds.

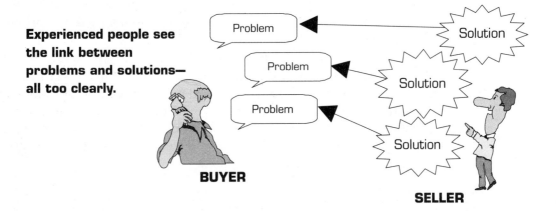

Experienced people see the link between problems and solutions—all too clearly.

Because experienced people see how the solution fits the buyer's problem they often jump quickly to solutions before the buyer is ready. In contrast, the most successful salespeople we studied held back and discussed the effects of the problem before talking about products or solutions. Questions about the effects or consequences of a buyer's problem are called Implication Questions. They are the most powerful of all sales questions because they help the buyer see that the problem is serious enough to justify the hassle and cost of a solution. Typical Implication Questions might be:

- *What effect do these problems have on your competitive position?*
- *Could that lead to an increase in your costs?*
- *How will this problem affect your people's productivity?*

Implication Questions like these are powerful because they induce pain. They build the consequences of the buyer's problems and, in so doing, make the buyer more anxious for a solution that will take the pain away. *That's why top salespeople hold back from early answers and instead ask Implication Questions. They skillfully build the pain. They create a stronger need before introducing their solutions.*

There's a simple exercise you can try for helping you to think about implications:

1. Choose a problem that you can solve really well, preferably one where you have a distinct competitive advantage.

2. Imagine that you are talking with a buyer who is the perfect candidate for your solution.

3. Now imagine that the buyer tells you, "I know you can solve this problem but I don't think it's serious enough to justify the effort and cost involved."

4. Think of the reasons why the buyer is wrong, why it *is* worth the effort or cost. These reasons are the implications that the buyer has not yet considered. In real life you should ask Implication Questions to draw these reasons out from the buyer. But, before you can ask Implication Questions, you need to have a clear idea of what the implications are likely to be. This exercise is a good way to uncover those implications.

Example

Problem Where You Have a Superior Solution	Assume the Buyer Says, "Sure but it's not worth the cost and hassle." Why Is the Buyer Wrong?
Our design software allows you to make design revisions much faster than you can with your existing design process.	• Design revisions are the main cause of slowdowns in the product development cycle, so that new products come to market late. • In today's competitive world a late product is a dead product. • The longer it takes to make revisions, the greater the overall design cost. • Competitors with shorter design cycles will eat your lunch. • Your best designers won't stick around if you can't provide them with the state-of-the-art tools they expect.

These reasons allow you to plan Implication Questions such as:

- *What will it do to your competitive position if the new product is late?*
- *What effect does the slowness of your revision process have on your best designers?*
- *If competitors have a faster revision process, what impact will that have?*

Try it with a product or service of your own:

Problem Where You Have a Superior Solution	Assume the Buyer Says, "Sure but it's not worth the cost and hassle." Why Is the Buyer Wrong?

A consultant who had struggled to ask Implication Questions and had found them very difficult once told us, "I just couldn't seem to get the idea until one day I got turned down by a client when I *knew* that what I was suggesting was the right answer. This client was just plain wrong. All the reasons why he was wrong flashed through my head and then I realized that each reason was an implication that I hadn't asked about. So I took a deep breath and said, 'Before you turn this idea down, could I ask you a few questions?' Then I translated the reasons why he was wrong into some 'what would happen if …' questions. It turned things around and I won the business."

Many other people have reported similar experiences—their ability to ask Implication Questions started from a list of reasons why the buyer was wrong—which is why we designed this exercise.

Implication Questions at a Glance

DEFINITION:	Asking about the consequences or effects of a buyer's problems, difficulties, or dissatisfactions.
EXAMPLES:	*What effect does that problem have on output?*
	Could that lead to added costs?
IMPACT:	The most powerful of all SPIN® questions. Top salespeople ask lots of Implication Questions.
ADVICE:	These questions are the hardest to ask. Read the chapter on Implication Questions and plan them carefully before key calls.

Implication Questions

Need-payoff Questions

The final type of question used by successful salespeople asks about the value or usefulness of a solution. We call these Need-payoff Questions—an inelegant label, but we couldn't find a better word beginning with *N* to give us the acronym SPIN®. Typical Need-payoff Questions include:

- *Why is it important to solve this problem?*
- *Is there any other way this solution would help?*
- *How much would you save if we could speed this operation by 20 percent?*

The common factor in questions like these is that—unlike Situation, Problem, and Implication Questions—they focus on solutions. Because of this solution focus, buyers rate calls that are high in Need-payoff Questions as positive, constructive, and useful.

Need-payoff Questions are often the mirror image of Implication Questions. So, for example, a buyer might have a problem that the present system is unreliable. One way to explore the problem might be to ask an Implication Question such as, *"Could that unreliability create waste that adds to your costs?"* But the same idea could equally well be explored using a Need-payoff Question like, *"If you had better reliability, wouldn't that cut waste and reduce costs?"* Either way is valid and skilled salespeople usually use a mixture of Implication and Need-payoff Questions to explore the consequences of problems and solutions.

Need-payoff Questions, however, are much more than a positive way to ask about implications. They have a unique function in that they get the buyer to tell you about the benefits your solution offers, rather than forcing you to explain the benefits to the buyer. So, for example, instead of saying, *"Our faster system will help you by reducing the present production bottleneck,"* you might ask the Need-payoff Question, *"How would our faster system help you?"* In response, the buyer can tell *you* that a faster machine would help with the bottleneck. By getting buyers to talk about the benefits you offer, you can have greater impact, while sounding a lot less pushy.

The idea of using questions to get the buyer to tell you about your benefits is a powerful one. Try it out by generating some examples of your own like the following ones.

Potential Benefit Your Product or Service Offers	Need-payoff Question to Get the Buyer to Tell You the Benefit
Our system is easy to use.	*What advantages would you see from a system that could be used by untrained operators?*
There's a very short set-up time.	*If you could cut your present setup time by half, what would that do to your output?*
We have attractive leasing terms.	*Would it help your cash position if you could get a new system without paying capital costs?*
And we offer on-line diagnostics.	*How would it help to have on-line diagnostics?*

Try it with your own example:

Potential Benefit Your Product or Service Offers	Need-payoff Question to Get the Buyer to Tell You the Benefit

It's often said that selling is not about convincing buyers but about creating the right conditions to allow buyers to convince themselves. There's truth in that saying. Need-payoff Questions can play a powerful role in setting up the conditions that let buyers tell you the benefits and, in so doing, convince themselves. When we were doing our initial research that led to the SPIN® model, we had an opportunity to travel with the top salespeople from a division of Xerox. We found that the Xerox people seemed to have buyers who often said things like, "Let me tell you another way in which Xerox can help me...." We used to joke that it wasn't that they were great salespeople, it was just that they had such great customers. Closer analysis showed that the reason why the Xerox buyers were coming up with so many ways in which Xerox products could help them was that these top Xerox salespeople were asking Need-payoff Questions that encouraged their buyers to talk about the benefits Xerox could offer.

Need-payoff Questions at a Glance

Need-payoff Questions	**DEFINITION:**	Asking about the value or usefulness of a proposed solution.
	EXAMPLES:	*How would a quieter printer help?*
		If we did that, how much could you save?
	IMPACT:	Versatile questions used a great deal by top salespeople. Positive impact on customers who rate calls high in Need-payoff Questions as helpful and constructive.
	ADVICE:	Use these questions to get buyers to tell *you* the benefits that your solution can offer.

Final Points on the SPIN® Model

High-level selling never works successfully if you try to sell by a rigid formula. Treat the SPIN® model as a formula and you'll fail. The model is a description of how successful people sell. It's backed by careful and extensive research—far and away the most comprehensive research into successful selling ever carried out. The model is broadly a sequence. Generally, for example, most sales discussions begin establishing some background information using Situation Questions. Then the seller usually uncovers one or more problems. Unless the buyer volunteers these problems, it's likely that the seller uncovers them using Problem Questions. As we've seen, top salespeople don't jump in with solutions at this point. They explore the problem; they build the pain a little. To do so, it's likely that they will ask Implication Questions. Finally the discussion turns to solutions, and that's where successful people ask Need-payoff Questions. So the questions of the SPIN® model are normally in sequence. But not in a rigid sequence. Nobody sells effectively by first asking all Situation Questions, then moving to all Problem Questions, and so forth. Flexibility is the hallmark of good selling. Treat the SPIN® model as a flexible road map for the call and it will help you as it has helped thousands of others.

3
Check It Out!

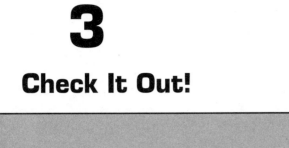

Good morning ...
Can I ask you a few
questions?

Questions? You
can ask questions,
but do I have to
give you answers?

Hello, Ms. Brodie.
Can I sell you
something today?

Who called this
meeting, anyway?

Which comes first,
the Situation or the
Problem?

Let me tell you all
about our great
products ...

Do I have to listen
to this????

If you think you already know the SPIN® model but you're not sure, OR you've read *SPIN® Selling* but haven't tried SPIN® in the field yet, OR you've been trained in SPIN® but haven't been through the material for a while, then this chapter is for you.

The questions (and answers) in this chapter will help you decide how to focus your efforts as you use the rest of this book to refresh, develop, and hone your selling knowledge and skills.

So don't worry if you find any of these questions difficult. Use the results to point you toward your next steps in this book. As you work through each chapter, you'll add to and build on what you already know. And after you practice applying the concepts and methods to sample situations and to your own cases, the last exercise in each chapter gives you another chance to check your learning.

Every set of Questions in this chapter is followed by the corresponding set of Answers.

The following questions ask about selling in general. You'll find more information on these topics in Chapters 4, 6, and 7–9.

True or False

1. If you want to persuade, it's better to give information than to seek it.

2. Most people give more than they seek when they try to persuade.

3. Investigating a buyer's needs is an important part of most sales calls.

4. The key reason for asking questions in a sales call is to uncover and develop buyer needs.

5. Implied Needs are statements of wants or desires by the prospective buyer.

... And let me tell you another thing ...

ZZZZZZZ ...

Is each of the following an Implied Need (statement of a customer's problem) or an Explicit Need (statement of a customer's want or desire)?

Implied or Explicit

6. *My present system is too slow.*

7. *I'm looking for a machine with reduction and enlargement capability.*

8. *Filing space is a problem in this office.*

Answers are on the next page.

1. False   Not on your life! Few of us are persuaded by listening to the opinions of others. Research shows that giving your ideas, arguments, or opinions has a low impact on other people and rarely succeeds. It's hard to talk someone into accepting your point, especially if the decision is a big one. It's much more effective to ask questions that let people talk themselves into acceptance.

     Remember, questions are the secret of sales success. Studies show that high-performing salespeople ask more questions. If you don't ask questions, you won't sell effectively. This book will help you build your seeking skills.

2. True   It's sad, but true. Giving ideas, opinions, or arguments is the most common way people try to persuade each other. Giving is so much easier than seeking. So we get in the habit of persuading that way. Unfortunately, it doesn't work well. If you build a selling style based on seeking, you can be much more effective.

3. True   It's a *very* important part. More sales are lost by doing a poor job in this stage of the sale than for any other single reason. Handling the Investigating stage well is the biggest difference between successful and unsuccessful sellers. (To learn more about the stages of a sales call, read Chapter 4.)

4. True   The purpose of the Investigating stage of a sale is to uncover and develop buyer needs. Your client or customer becomes ready to buy by making those needs clear and strong. And you develop buyer needs by the questions you ask. (To find out how buyer needs develop, read Chapters 6–10.)

5. False   A buyer's needs don't start in the form of a want or desire. Implied Needs are a buyer's statements about a problem, difficulty, or dissatisfaction with the existing situation. The purpose of the Investigating stage is to ask questions that reveal Implied Needs and then *develop* them into statements of clear, strong wants and desires—in other words, into Explicit Needs. (Read Chapter 6 to learn all about Implied and Explicit Needs and why they matter.)

6. Implied   States a problem with the current system, not a want or desire.

7. Explicit   "I'm looking for …" is a statement of want, not about a problem or difficulty.

8. Implied   The need is stated in the form of a problem, not as a want or desire.

Now try some other questions. More information on these topics can be found in Chapters 4, 7, and 8.

True or False

1. When opening a call, it's important to describe the full details of your product so that the buyer knows exactly what you've got to offer.

2. The sign that you have opened a call correctly is that the buyer knows who you are, knows why you're there, and agrees that you should ask questions.

3. After you've opened a call, you should immediately ask Problem Questions to uncover needs.

4. The more Situation Questions you ask, the more likely the customer or client will be to buy.

So, Mr. Kent, have you had problems since telephone booths stopped being made?

Not at all. Why do you ask?

What? He must be an alien agent or something. I'd never admit that!

Situation or Problem Question

Which is a Situation Question and which a Problem Question?

5. *How many units do you use during an average month?* _____

6. *Are you satisfied with your current service contract?* _____

Answers are on the next page.

1. False A lot of people do this, but it won't help you get business. Why shouldn't you talk about your products or services at the start of a call? Because:

- Giving is less powerful than seeking. Telling the buyer about your product or service is a weak way to influence.

- Describing your product or service is the same as offering a solution too early, a common mistake that can negatively impact larger sales.

- Since you don't yet know what the buyer needs, your solution may be inappropriate.

- Describing your product or service too early often leads *buyers* to ask you questions, especially about price, creating unnecessary objections.

Just try to "set the scene" in your Opening, so that *you* can ask the questions.

2. True Every Opening needs to ensure that the buyer knows who you are, knows why you're there, and agrees to let you ask questions. Of course, if you already know the buyer, this may occur automatically. But with new prospects, you'll need to introduce yourself, explain why you're there, and get their okay to begin asking your SPIN® questions. (See Chapter 4.)

3. False It would be very risky to ask Problem Questions right after opening the call—unless the buyer has already opened by describing a problem to you. Few people are willing to admit to problems, especially to a stranger. Probing too soon for difficulties can cause buyers to deny or cover up problems. It's much better to start by asking a few neutral, fact-finding Situation Questions, and move on to Problem Questions after you understand the buyer's current business and operations. (Chapter 8 tells when to ask Problem Questions.)

4. False No way. If asking only Situation Questions got people to buy, how easy selling would be! But asking more than a few, well-focused Situation Questions makes the call less likely to succeed. (To learn why that is, and why most people ask too many Situation Questions, read Chapter 7.) In fact, asking Problem Questions and especially Implication Questions has a much more powerful impact on making the sale.

5. Situation Situation Questions ask for facts about the existing situation.

6. Problem Problem Questions ask about problems, difficulties and dissatisfactions with the existing situation. Asking if the buyer is satisfied is an indirect but effective way to probe for dissatisfaction.

Now the questions get a little harder. But don't worry if you don't get all the answers. That's why you're reading this book. Meanwhile, you'll find lots more in Chapters 8 and 9.

True or False

1. When the buyer states a problem, and it's one you can solve, you should immediately offer your solution. ☐

2. The purpose of Implication Questions is to extend and develop a buyer's perception of the consequences and effects of problems. ☐

3. The best time to ask Implication Questions is early in the call, before you've uncovered problems. ☐

4. Most people find it much harder to ask Implication Questions than to ask Problem Questions. ☐

Good morning, Mr. Rice. What are the implications of your problems today?

Good grief!!!

Problem or Implication Question

Distinguish Problem and Implication Questions.

5. *How hard is it to change the cartridges in your machine?* _____

6. *Has the poor output quality caused customer complaints?* _____

7. *If you've got a reliability problem, exactly how much extra is that costing you over a year's time?* _____

8. *Are you satisfied with the range of motion you're getting from the swing-arm?* _____

Answers are on the next page.

1. False No, no, no! It is tempting, when a buyer offers you a nice problem you can solve, to joyfully toss your solution straight into the buyer's arms. What's wrong with wanting to help—selling your solution at the same time? Simply put, it doesn't work. In fact, giving your solution too soon can *lose* you the sale. This is such a common mistake that we'll warn you about it frequently.

Fundamentally, *the impact of a solution depends on the size of the buyer's need.* Successful sellers know that they must develop the buyer's Implied Needs (problems) into strong clear Explicit Needs, before offering solutions.

2. True When you offer solutions, the buyer's need stops growing. So you must first find a way to develop the buyer's perception of the size and significance of a problem before you start discussing your answers. The best way to do this is through your questions. Implication Questions are the most effective way to help a buyer understand the full consequences and effects of problems. (See Chapter 9 to learn more about using Implication Questions.)

3. False By their very nature, you can't ask Implication Questions until a problem has been uncovered. Asking Problem Questions helps you and the buyer understand what problems, dissatisfactions, and difficulties the buyer has. Implication Questions are asked after Problem Questions, so that the buyer becomes more aware of their seriousness and significance. (See Chapter 8 for more on Problem Questions.)

4. True Unfortunately, Implication Questions are much harder to ask than Situation or Problem Questions. They require planning and business knowledge, so that you can understand why certain problems would be important and what factors might cause them to be more significant than the buyer might realize. You also need to know what kinds of problems your products or services can solve, so you can focus on developing those Implied Needs.

5. Problem Here the seller is probing directly for an Implied Need.

6. Implication In contrast to question 5, this question seeks to extend or develop a problem that's already been identified by the buyer.

7. Implication This question develops a problem by asking the buyer to quantify it.

8. Problem This question simply probes for an area of difficulty.

Moving right along, only one part to go after this. You'll find more information on the topic in Chapter 10.

True or False

1. The purpose of Need-payoff Questions is to move the buyer's attention away from problems and focus it on solutions and their value.

2. Need-payoff Questions should not be asked until after the buyer's problems have been identified and developed.

3. You should never ask Need-payoff Questions after the buyer has expressed Explicit Needs.

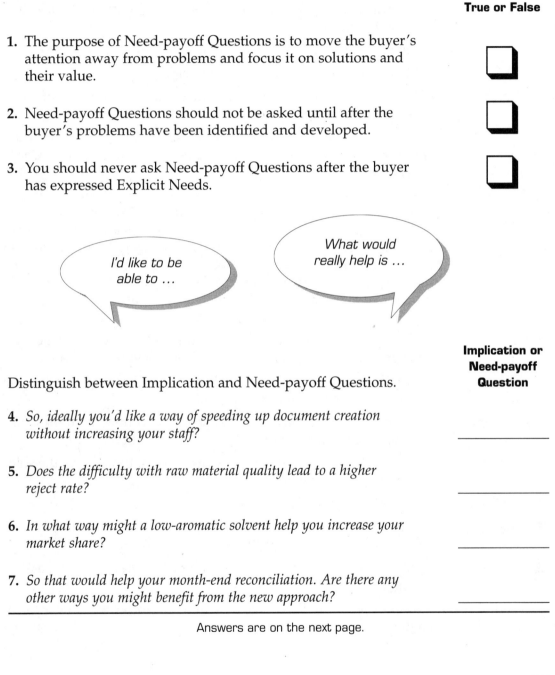

> I'd like to be able to ...

> What would really help is ...

Distinguish between Implication and Need-payoff Questions.

Implication or Need-payoff Question

4. *So, ideally you'd like a way of speeding up document creation without increasing your staff?*

5. *Does the difficulty with raw material quality lead to a higher reject rate?*

6. *In what way might a low-aromatic solvent help you increase your market share?*

7. *So that would help your month-end reconciliation. Are there any other ways you might benefit from the new approach?*

Answers are on the next page.

1. True   It's not very effective to talk about solutions when the buyer's mind is still on problems. So you need to shift the buyer's attention. How? By asking questions that get the buyer to start thinking about the *value* or *usefulness of a solution*. Need-payoff Questions do just that. They invite the buyer to:

- *Switch attention* from the problem to the solution.

- *Think about* how the solution could help.

- *Describe to you* the ways your product or service could be of value or use to the buyer.

No wonder Need-payoff Questions are so powerful in selling: They get the buyer to tell you about the Benefits you can offer. (See Chapter 11 as well as Chapter 10.)

2. True   Asking Need-payoff Questions too early is a very common mistake. There's danger in questions like, *"Wouldn't a faster system be useful?"* or *"In your kind of operation, wouldn't it pay you to adopt our method?"* If asked too early in the call, the buyer could say "yes" but feel no real interest or commitment. It's also risky to focus on solutions before the buyer has recognized a problem and its significance. Asking Need-payoff Questions is much more effective after you've explored the buyer's problems and their implications.

3. False   On the contrary, some of the best Need-payoff Questions come after an Explicit Need has been expressed. Need-payoff Questions can:

- *Identify* the existence of an Explicit Need by asking whether the buyer wants or is interested in a solution.

- *Clarify* the Explicit Need by asking why and how the need is important, or by quantifying the value of a solution.

- *Extend* the value of a solution by discovering other ways the solution might help the buyer.

4. Need-payoff   Seeks to *identify* the Explicit Need.

5. Implication   The question is problem-centered and develops the Implied Need before moving toward a solution.

6. Need-payoff   In contrast to question 5, this is a solution-centered question, asking the buyer to *clarify* the areas of payoff.

7. Need-payoff   This example shows how Need-payoff Questions can *extend* areas of payoff.

Almost there. Chapter 11 gives you the whole scoop on Demonstrating Capability, and Chapter 4 fills you in on Obtaining Commitment from a buyer.

True or False

1. The more Features you can describe to a buyer during the call, the more likely you will be to make the sale.

2. Benefits are the most powerful way you can describe your solutions to buyers.

3. Benefits show how a product or service can meet a buyer's Implied Need.

4. Objections are a sign that the buyer is interested. So the more objections you get from the buyer, the better your chances of making a sale.

5. Asking a lot of Implication and Need-payoff Questions will reduce the number of objections the buyer raises.

When's this turkey going to make a commitment?

When's this jerk going to ask for a commitment?

6. Never take the initiative by asking the buyer for a commitment; always let the sale close itself.

7. The more you use closing techniques during a sales call, the more likely you are to make the sale.

Answers are on the next page.

1. False   The number of Features you describe has little impact on the outcome of the sale. In fact, research shows that there are generally more Features given in calls that fail than in those that succeed. It's far better to spend time *developing buyer needs* with Problem, Implication, and Need-payoff Questions and *making Benefits* to show how you can meet the Explicit Needs you've developed. (See Chapter 11 for more on questions 1 through 5.)

2. True   Benefits are absolutely the most powerful way to describe your products or services to buyers. The key to success in selling is the ability to *uncover* Implied Needs using Situation and Problem Questions, *develop* them into Explicit Needs using Implication and Need-payoff Questions, and then *satisfy* those Explicit Needs with Benefits.

3. False   Be careful: Benefits show how a product or service can meet an *Explicit Need* expressed by the buyer. An Implied Need is only a half-developed need. First you have to build the seriousness of the need so that your buyer expresses a clear strong desire for a solution.

4. False   The more objections you get, the *worse* your chances of making a sale. Objections are barriers between you and the buyer, and research shows that they're most often caused by poor selling skills. Successful sellers put their emphasis on *preventing objections* rather than handling objections.

5. True   By using Implication and Need-payoff Questions to develop Explicit Needs, you can reduce the number of objections you receive and increase your chances of making a sale. The key is to develop strong Explicit Needs in the buyer before you offer your solution. (Chapter 11 explains the difference between "Benefits," which help make a sale, and "Advantages," which raise objections.)

6. False   The overuse of closing techniques can certainly hurt your selling. But the total absence of closing is even more damaging. The sale won't close itself; so you've got to take the initiative. Research shows that it's most successful to close once per call, after you've effectively developed your buyer's needs.

7. False   Many experienced sellers think that frequent use of closing techniques improves your sales success, but research shows the opposite: Increasing the number of closes in a call actually reduces your success rate. If you haven't developed your buyer's needs, *no* closing technique can guarantee you a sale. (See Chapter 4 for more on Obtaining Commitment.)

4

Four Stages of a Sales Call

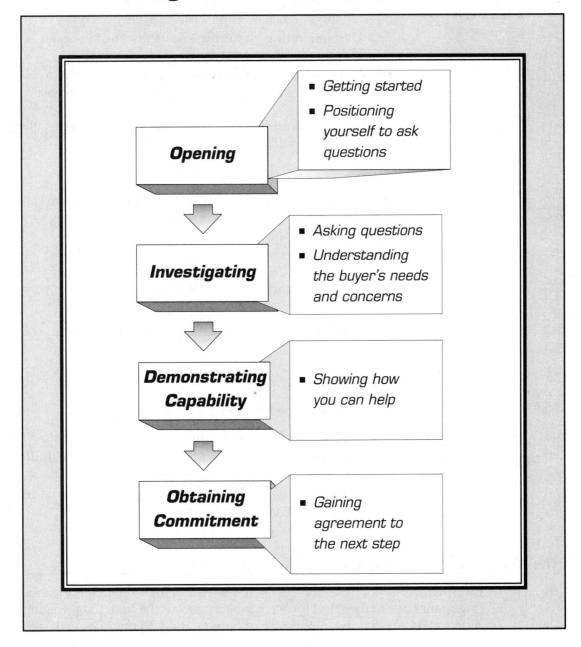

- Getting started
- Positioning yourself to ask questions

Opening

- Asking questions
- Understanding the buyer's needs and concerns

Investigating

- Showing how you can help

Demonstrating Capability

- Gaining agreement to the next step

Obtaining Commitment

Overview

> **What are the four stages of a sales call?**

1. **Opening**—the preliminaries, including introductions and beginning the conversation.
2. **Investigating**—uncovering, clarifying, and developing the buyer's needs.
3. **Demonstrating Capability**—establishing how your solution meets buyer needs.
4. **Obtaining Commitment**—securing agreement to an action that moves the sale forward toward purchase.

> **Which is most important?**

Research evidence shows that the Investigating stage is the most crucial to success in large or complex sales.

Almost all sales, from the simplest to the most sophisticated, go through the same four stages, leading to the same ultimate results or outcomes:

- An **Order** or *win*—where there is a commitment to buy.
- A **No-sale** or *loss*—where there is a refusal to buy.

But in large or complex sales calls, because of the time required to complete the sale, there may also be two other interim outcomes:

- An **Advance**—where there is buyer agreement on an action that moves the sale forward.
- A **Continuation**—where there is no buyer agreement on an action that would move the sale forward.

So, in large or complex sales:

> **So what does that really mean?**

- The whole cycle usually requires multiple calls.
- Success in Obtaining Commitment depends on skillfully conducting the Investigating stage.
- It's crucial to set realistic call objectives and achieve call outcomes that actively move the sale forward.

The Most Important Stage in a Sale

Research, including the SPIN® research, shows that Investigating is the most important stage of the sale. However, for generations the traditional wisdom didn't acknowledge the importance of Investigating. Many sales managers swore that Obtaining Commitment—"closing"—had to be most important.

In *small* sales, there is some evidence to suggest that "if you can't close, you can't sell." But in *large* and *complex* sales, success depends, more than anything else, on the skills used by the seller in the Investigating stage.

What exactly is Investigating? In a sales context, Investigating means systematically discovering, exploring, clarifying, and understanding the buyer's business needs and problems. And to investigate, you must ask questions.

Questions, Questions, All Kinds of Questions

Questions are the most effective form of verbal behavior you can use to persuade. And that's not just in selling. Multiple research studies have overwhelmingly shown that more questions are asked in successful negotiations, management interactions, performance interviews, group discussions, and other interactions than in unsuccessful ones.

Huthwaite's research went further. We examined scientifically, for example, the standard assumption that "open" questions are better for selling than "closed" questions. First, let's define each:

- **Closed questions** can be answered with a single word, often "yes" or "no."
- **Open questions** require longer, more descriptive answers, often taking the form of *"Could you tell me something about ...?"* or *"Why is that important to you ...?"*

Since open questions get the buyer talking, conventional wisdom has been that there ought to be a connection to successful selling. Our studies found, however, that there is no link between whether questions are open or closed and successful selling.

But we did find that certain other kinds of questions *are* linked directly to successful selling when asked in a particular sequence. As we've seen, those are the SPIN® questions.

Why the Investigating Stage Is So Important

People purchase something to meet needs or resolve problems. They decide to buy when the pain of the problem and desire for a solution have been built to the point where they are greater than the cost of the solution. And it's the Investigating stage where SPIN® questions are used to help you to uncover and develop your buyer's problems.

Opening the Call

In larger sales, less is known about the Opening stage of the call than the other stages for a simple reason: Most larger sales involve existing customers or clients, where buyers and sellers are already acquainted. Less than 5 percent of meetings that major account sellers have are first calls with new customers, but some research data does exist for these kinds of Openings.

The book *SPIN® Selling* describes how and why certain traditional methods for opening a call may work in small sales but don't for larger sales (pages 137–143). One such approach is the use of an "opening benefits statement." In this approach, the seller opens with a statement about how the product or service could help the buyer. In very brief calls, that are less than 10 minutes long, an opening benefits statement may help engage the buyer's interest in your product or service. But in longer calls—and an average business-to-business sales call lasts 40 minutes—there is no link between the success of the sale and using an opening benefits statement. In fact, it can be risky.

Don't Introduce Your Solution Too Soon!

One of the biggest traps inexperienced sellers fall into is introducing their solution too early. It's so tempting and so common that we'll caution you frequently about it. *What our research has repeatedly shown is that successful sellers don't talk about their products, services, or the benefits of their solution until **late in the sales call.***

Since making an opening benefit statement is an early (very early!) way of introducing your product or service, it is very likely to sabotage your call. Why? Because:

- It forces the seller to talk about product or service details *before building value.*
- It allows the *buyer* to ask the questions and take control of the discussion.

The Purpose of Opening

The purpose of Opening is to gain the buyer's agreement for you to ask questions—to move on to the Investigating stage.

A good opening should establish a *buyer-centered* purpose. What does this mean? It means focusing on the buyer's concerns, rather than on your product or service. It also means being flexible—considering factors such as who set up the meeting, how well you know the client or customer, and what time constraints exist.

Although you also need to communicate who you are and why you're there (*not* by giving details of your product or service), as well as to establish a basis for asking your SPIN® questions, it's important to stay focused on the buyer's concerns, rather than your own needs. Being buyer-centered helps establish trust and receptivity, and builds your credibility.

Opening Your Calls Effectively

1. **Get down to business quickly.** While you need to respect the norms of the organization and culture, a greater danger is wasting the time of a busy executive. As a general rule, spend as little time as necessary on the Opening.

2. **Don't talk about solutions too soon.** Using an opening benefits statement is an example of prematurely introducing your solution. It's crucial to develop the buyer's needs and build value before you offer a solution or talk about your capabilities. Talking about solutions too soon causes objections and reduces the likelihood of a sale.

3. **Concentrate on questions.** Don't worry too much about appearing smooth or polished in the preliminaries of the call. Plan some appropriate questions ahead of the meeting and use the time in the Opening stage to gain the buyer's consent to move forward to the Investigating stage. If you find that the buyer is asking the questions—that you're being asked for facts and explanations—you'll need to vary the way you open calls to establish your role as questioner during this stage.

It will help if you practice doing 30-second openings until you're confident you've covered the key points without sounding "automatic." The best test of whether you're being effective in the Opening stage is how readily the buyer becomes receptive to answering your questions.

The SPIN® Questions and the Investigating Stage

Since the Investigating stage has the most impact on the buyer's decision to purchase your product or service, using the SPIN® questions effectively is, as you'll see, the core of successful face-to-face selling. The next chapters will show you how to use SPIN® questions during the Investigating stage to uncover, clarify, and develop buyer needs.

Demonstrating Capability

Sooner or later you have to demonstrate that you have a solution that can help solve the buyer's problems. You can use a variety of methods to demonstrate the value of your solution, but what may work in simple sales *won't* work as the size or complexity of the sale increases. One example is that in large sales, introducing your solution *later* is clearly more effective than doing it sooner. Chapter 10 covers how Need-payoff Questions are used during this stage to help the buyer identify the benefits and, by extension, the value of your solution. Chapter 11 is devoted to Demonstrating Capability.

Obtaining Commitment

When *SPIN® Selling* was first published, common wisdom held strongly that Obtaining Commitment—closing—was the most important stage of a sale. Chapter 2 of that book describes the struggles we went through to show conclusively that the traditional wisdom about the importance of closing was just plain wrong.

In large or complex sales, what is most important is how sellers handle the Investigating stage.

SPIN® Selling has helped people understand how traditional closing techniques are indeed ineffective or have a negative impact when:

- The sale is large or complex, or when it involves high-value goods or services.
- Selling to a sophisticated customer or client—for example, a professional buyer.
- There is a continuing relationship after the sale.

SPIN® Selling not only points out the dangers of closing; it also points out that you must still obtain some kind of commitment from the buyer, or you won't have a sale. In a simple sale, either you get a commitment to buy, an Order, or the prospect refuses to buy and you have a No-sale. Either way, it's relatively easy and quick to tell if you have a successful sale. But larger, complex sales are very different. In larger sales the key is to obtain the right commitment.

Obtaining the RIGHT Commitment

Large sales can involve many individual calls and sometimes take years to complete. In major account sales, fewer than 10 percent of calls actually result in an Order or a No-sale. With neither an outright rejection or a contract in hand, how can you tell if a call is successful? What other call outcomes might define success versus failure in large or complex sales?

The starting point for Obtaining Commitment in these kinds of sales is determining the level of commitment that would make the call a success.

Call Outcomes

In simple sales, there are really just two possible call outcomes: You get either an Order or a No-sale. Large or complex sales are different. It may take months or years to get the Order. So you need to be able to identify other successful and unsuccessful call outcomes along the way.

In large sales, if an individual call results in an action that moves you closer to a sale—what we call an *Advance*—it is a successful outcome. The key

Call outcomes

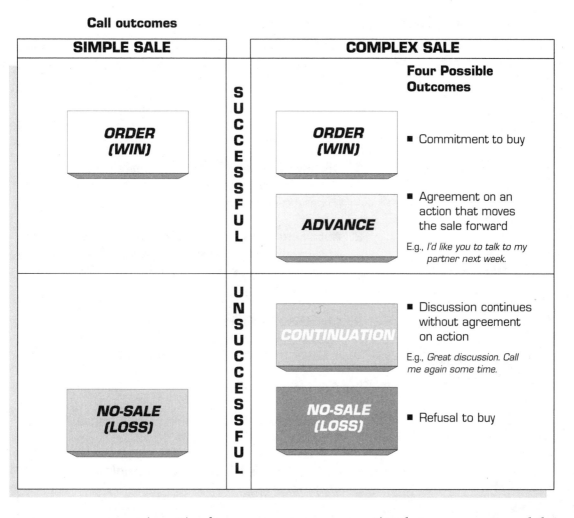

measure is getting buyer agreement on *an action that moves you toward the sale.* The "action" may be taken by either the buyer or the seller. But a buyer action always makes a clearer and stronger Advance, because it shows the buyer's commitment to moving the sale forward, e.g., the buyer agrees to attend a demo or arrange a meeting for the seller with other decision makers. A buyer's request for a proposal would not be a clear Advance unless the *buyer* also agrees to take some action that moves the sale forward, such as reviewing the selection criteria before you write the proposal or discussing a draft proposal before final submission.

The outcome of a call that does not reach agreement on action that moves the sale forward—a *Continuation*—is unsuccessful, no matter how pleasant or complimentary the buyer seems.

Obtaining Commitment—a Summary

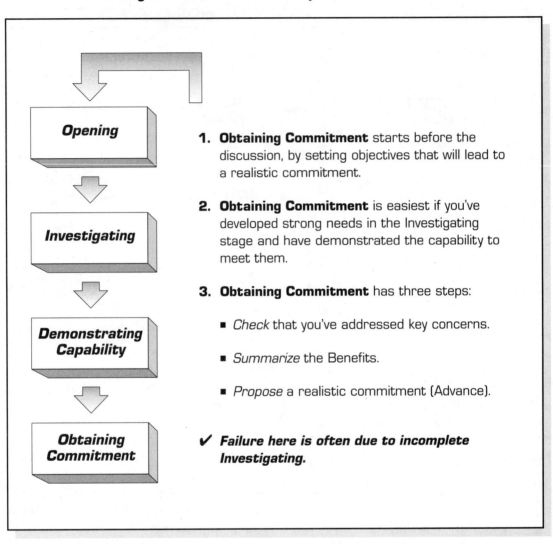

1. **Obtaining Commitment** starts before the discussion, by setting objectives that will lead to a realistic commitment.

2. **Obtaining Commitment** is easiest if you've developed strong needs in the Investigating stage and have demonstrated the capability to meet them.

3. **Obtaining Commitment** has three steps:

   - *Check* that you've addressed key concerns.

   - *Summarize* the Benefits.

   - *Propose* a realistic commitment (Advance).

   ✔ *Failure here is often due to incomplete Investigating.*

Top sellers close more calls, more effectively, by:

   ✔ Turning Continuations into Advances.
   ✔ Understanding what kind of Advance can make the call successful.
   ✔ Setting realistic closing objectives that move the sale forward.

Planning Advances

Top sellers reach their ultimate goals by consistently planning and conducting calls that move the sale forward in steps. What exactly do they do? They start by brainstorming to identify the widest variety of Advances that would move them toward a sale. Really skilled sellers then select those ingenious small actions that the buyer is likely to agree to. Having determined an array of useful Advances, the seller is ready to set a realistic call objective, but will have alternative actions to propose as needed for the actual visit. This approach increases the likelihood that the visit will result in an Advance.

Example

The Seller provides corporations with mobile telephone system packages that include equipment, repair service, an array of calling plans, voicemail, and other services. The customer contact is a senior project manager in the company's telecommunications department, and is one member of a six-member selection team (chaired by the department director) that will make the final purchasing decision. The customer has six regional sites in this country. The seller is planning for the second meeting with this contact.

Possible Advances:

- Meet the department director, using our vice-president sales to set up the meeting.
- Get the project manager to call two of our satisfied customers.
- Get a meeting arranged with all the members of the selection team.
- Set up introduction to the regional sales manager during Atlanta Telecom Fair.
- Get their list of vendor selection criteria.
- Get contact to attend a demo at our office.
- Get contact to propose a pilot field test to other selection team members.
- Get an introduction to other department heads.

Less successful sellers get more Continuations, where skilled sellers get Advances. How does that happen?

Many less successful salespeople are content with objectives like "collect info about the customer," "build rapport with the buyer," or "get buyer to say they like our system." There's nothing wrong with objectives like this. It's always good to find out more and build relationships. But, by themselves, objectives like these don't have action that moves the sale forward. They're Continuations. Selling requires more. It needs action—an Advance—to move the sale forward.

Practice Brainstorming Possible Advances

1. Select a customer or client of yours that you are scheduled to visit in the next couple of weeks.

2. Based on the current stage you are in of the sales cycle, and using your existing knowledge of your buyer's needs, brainstorm potential Advances. Go for quantity and variety. Include as many actions as possible that, if agreed to by the buyer, could move the sale forward.

3. List the possible Advances you come up with in the following space:

Background Notes on Customer	
Possible Advances	**Sure It's an Advance, Not a Continuation?**
▪	☐
▪	☐
▪	☐
▪	☐
▪	☐

4. Check each Advance to make sure it has a forward action. Otherwise it's just a Continuation.

5. Choose the Advance that involves the highest realistic action you think you can achieve. Make this the Call Objective for your visit. Highlight some fallback alternatives to offer as needed.

6. After the visit, review the actual call outcome. Did you get the Advance?

CHECK YOURSELF—CALL OUTCOMES

Are you clear about the possible call outcomes? Try to identify each of the following as either an *Order/Sale, Advance, Continuation,* or *No-sale.*

Call Outcome

1. *I'll cut a purchase order today so we can start right away.* _____

2. *No. Although we liked what you showed us, we've decided to go with Broad Associates.* _____

3. *I like what you've got to offer, and I enjoyed your presentation.* _____

4. *Let's meet again to continue this discussion sometime next month.* _____

5. *I can't make the decision alone, but I'll arrange for you to meet my partner next week.* _____

6. *We'll think about it and probably call you in the next few months.* _____

7. *If you could include those schedule modifications in your proposal, I'll present it to my associates.* _____

8. *All I need is my accountant's OK. We'll review it against our financial criteria and, if it passes, then you've got a deal.* _____

9. *We really need to see the system in action. Can you arrange a local demonstration for me and my production manager next Tuesday?* _____

Answers are on the next page.

1. Sale	If the buyer is prepared to complete the paperwork, there's not much doubt you've won the order.
2. No-sale	The client or customer has given you a clear statement that they are not buying from you.
3. Continuation	It's certainly nice of the buyer to say those things. But because there's no action involved that might progress the sale, this can only be a Continuation.
4. Continuation	Agreement to another meeting by itself, with no action, just continues the sale, rather than moving it toward a decision to buy. If, for example, the person added, "I'll bring one of the other vice-presidents from the selection committee," then this would be an Advance.
5. Advance	There is an action, a meeting with the partner, which advances the sale toward a decision to buy.
6. Continuation	The door isn't closed, but it could be a typical brush-off to get rid of the seller without actually saying "no sale." "Thinking about it" in this case is not an action, and does not progress the sale.
7. Advance	Here the buyer is proposing two actions: one for the seller (to include items in the proposal) and one for the buyer (to present the proposal to associates).
8. Advance	This is *not* an Order or sale, nor is it a "99 percent definite" kind of promise. Unless there's an unshakable commitment to sign, you should downgrade this kind of statement to an Advance.
9. Advance	The buyer is proposing three actions. In this case, the seller's action is to arrange a demo/site visit, and the buyer's two actions are to attend the demo and bring the production manager.

5
Putting **SPIN®** to Work

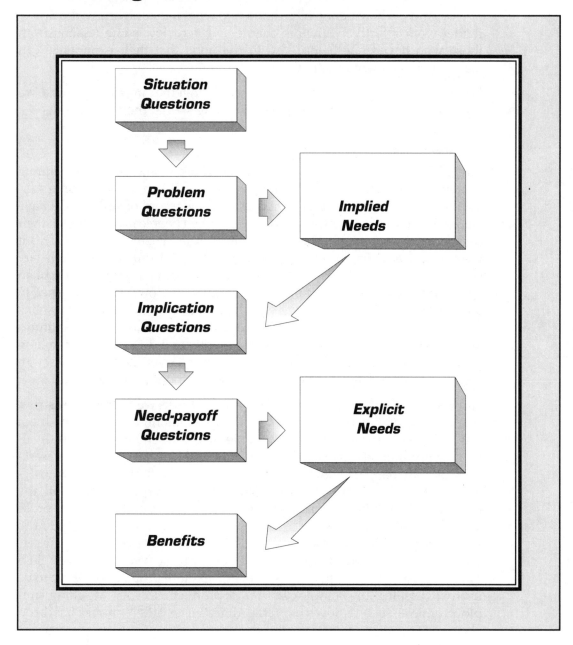

The Good News and the Bad News

More than a million people across the world have been trained to use the SPIN® model to help them sell more effectively. As you'd expect from such a large number, there have been spectacular stories of success, a few tales of woe, and a whole bunch of insights into what it takes to make the SPIN® model work effectively. In this chapter we'll review some lessons from those who have gone before you in the hope that their experience can make the implementation path easier for you.

If we had a cross section of all these people together in one place and we asked them to sum up their experiences, here's what they would say.

The Good News

The good news is that the model works. There would be overwhelming agreement that, whether you're selling in Tulsa or Tokyo, in Athens or in Amsterdam, the SPIN® questions have a tested track record of success. We have studies from over 30 countries to show that, when people use the model, their sales increase as a result. The large business sale, wherever in the world it takes place, has similarities that outweigh cultural differences. There are some cultural twists. For example, in Japan it's much harder to ask Problem Questions without appearing impolite or obtrusive. However, when asked in an indirect way that is consistent with Japanese culture, Problem Questions are very successful. They are equally useful questions to ask in other cultures where problems can be uncovered more bluntly and directly. So our million participants tell us that SPIN® questions work all over the world, although there are some differences in how to ask the questions effectively.

Another piece of good news is that the model works well across industries. Banks use it and so do bakeries. Consulting firms find that it helps them sell their services; construction companies use it to sell huge projects. In almost every industry you can imagine, the SPIN® model is being successfully used by people to uncover and develop needs. To those of us who developed the model, this is gratifying news but not surprising. After all, the common factor about complex products or services is that they solve problems for buyers. Whether we're talking about a consulting engagement to reengineer a process, a product to unclog drains, or a telephone repair service, the common link is that each solves a problem for the buyer. So a model that helps uncover, understand, and explore problems is likely to be useful for selling any complex service or product. How about selling simple products, such as low-cost retail items? The SPIN® model has been used by some retail stores to sell higher-priced goods such as furniture and we've had reports that it works well. We've also seen it used to sell simple services such as low-end banking products like savings accounts. However, to be frank, although the model can work well, it may be overkill. It's possible to sell simpler, one-call transactional products without the level of sophistication that the SPIN® model involves.

So the good news is that the SPIN® model:

- Has proved to be a versatile sales tool.
- Works across cultures.
- Applies across industries.
- Is equally applicable to selling services or selling products.

The Bad News

Then what's the bad news? Our million users would tell you in one voice: It's a lot harder than it seems. SPIN® isn't a magic pill that you can take and turn yourself into an instant sales success. It's hard work. One of the immutable laws of business is that there's always a link between risk and reward. The more rewarding the outcome, the tougher it is to obtain. If SPIN® questions were simple and automatic, then everyone would be using them already, and there would be no competitive advantage from the model. The reality is that good questioning is a complex skill that takes years of practice to master fully. As a result, many people who started out with enthusiasm have given up along the way. Like any other endeavor that's harder than it first seems, there's a high percentage of dropouts, particularly from people who are trying to learn the skills on their own without the help of systematic training or a coach. It's like that exercise program: You know you should get fit, you know that it will be good for you, but a week into it and you're experiencing all of the pain and none of the benefits. So you give up. There are many people—altogether too many—who have taken the SPIN® exercise program and have relapsed into the slothful habit of taking up too much air time with their buyers, the laziness of telling rather than asking, the indiscipline of jumping in with solutions before the problem has been understood and explored.

What can we learn from all those who have struggled to master the SPIN® model and to make it work for them? What are the lessons from those who started the fitness program but gave it up? Even more important, what can we learn from those who continued to work on the model and who are now fit, trim, and making more sales as a result?

The #1 Lesson—Planning

One lesson outweighs all others. To sell well, you must plan well. The first secret of success in implementing the SPIN® model is to invest in planning. If we had to design a slogan to put on the obligatory T-shirts that every company gives out at sales conferences, it would say this:

Planning, in the complex selling world of today, has to be much more than an anxiety attack in the elevator on the way up to the buyer's office. It has to be more than a few random thoughts to start the conversation going. Planning has to be a systematic and purposeful activity that makes the sales call work. Without good planning there is no good selling. The principal reason why many people find the SPIN® model difficult to execute is that either they haven't planned at all or they haven't planned well.

Over and over again, people tell us that the breakthrough that made them more successful in their selling was an understanding of the importance of planning sales calls and how to do it. Chapter 12 focuses on planning. Read it carefully. If you can plan well, you're already more than half way to selling well. As one person from a small consulting company told us:

> *At first I made the mistake of thinking that the SPIN® model was only about selling. It was something you didn't use, or even think about, until you were in there face-to-face with a prospective client. The big insight for me was to see SPIN® as a planning tool. That's when things really started to go well.*

Problem-Solving Orientation

Planning is the crucial first step for putting the SPIN® model into practice. A close second, for most people, is shifting their perspective away from their products and services toward a new perspective based on a problem-solving orientation. What does this mean? One of the early implementations of the SPIN® model was in Xerox Corporation, where we had a nice example of how powerful it can be to think of products in terms of the problems they solve.

Case: A Picture Can Be Worth a Million Dollars

In the early days of fax machines, they were called telecopiers. There weren't many sold because they were so expensive—in the $25,000–30,000 price bracket. Xerox was a telecopier pioneer and offered the first range of commercially available machines. Sales were flat because it was hard to compete with the much more widely used telex and teletype machines on the market that were available at a fraction of the cost. So it looked as if this technological breakthrough was going nowhere fast. We met with a group of Xerox telecopier salespeople and asked them to talk about what it was that they were selling. They told us a lot about transmission rates, answerback capabilities, remote auto operation, and the like. In other words, they told us about the product.

We trained a group in SPIN® selling methods and we helped put together a new approach to the product, thinking of it in terms of the problems it solved for customers. One of the interesting ideas that came from this approach was that a telecopier solved one problem that a telex machine couldn't: It was able to send a picture or a diagram, not just text. So we asked which customers were likely to have problems that could be solved only by sending a picture. After some thought, the group came up with a list that included police departments, universities, hospitals, and oil companies.

The oil company case was particularly interesting. One member of the group had read that British Petroleum was exploring the North Sea oil fields, taking seismographic and other readings. Twice a day a helicopter flew out to the drilling platforms to collect the data and bring it back to shore, where the geologists interpreted it. Because the seismographic readings were in the form of complex charts, there was no way that the information could be put into words and sent to shore by telephone or telex. "Just think," said the telecopier team member, "if they had telecopiers on the rigs, then they wouldn't need the helicopter runs. They could send the charts ashore quicker and at a fraction of the cost." Within a week of the idea, several sales were made to BP and other oil companies. These sales were worth hundreds of thousands of dollars, and they saved the oil companies many times that amount.

The breakthrough was a simple one: thinking of a product in terms of the problems it solved.

Try It Out

Thinking about your products in problem-solving terms is an important step towards successfully using the SPIN® model. It's not always as easy as it sounds. Try it.

1. Take a product or service that you offer.

2. Choose one specific type of buyer who might purchase the product or service. Preferably, choose a buyer type to whom you would like to make more sales than you are making right now.

3. List the Features, or characteristics, of the product/service. Pay particular attention to Features that competitively differentiate you or your product superiority.

4. For each Feature, list specific problems that it could solve for the specific buyer type that you have chosen.

Example

Product or Service: *Micropump*   **Buyer Type:** *Research laboratory*

Characteristic of Product/Service	*Problems It Solves for This Buyer*
Exact chamber capacity	Labs find it hard to measure the exact amount of additive in formulations. Precise chamber capacity lets them do this without additional meters or instrumentation.
Titanium construction	Conventional steel pumps are damaged by corrosive liquids such as concentrated acids. The Micropump can handle corrosives that would otherwise have to be metered manually with risk of spillage.
Silent operation	Noise is a problem in labs where technicians often dictate notes and readings of results. The low noise of Micropump makes it easier to dictate instrument readings and notes.
Modular construction	Cleaning conventional pumps takes up to half an hour. Micropump's modular construction allows cleaning in less than one minute, saving time and cost.

Your Turn

Now try it with a product or service of your own.

Product or Service: _____   **Buyer Type:** _____

Characteristics of Product/Service	Problems It Solves for This Buyer

Now check the list of problems that you can solve for your chosen buyer:

- Did you describe *specific* problems that you can solve? [like *"low noise makes it easier for technicians to dictate instrument readings and notes"* rather than *"quiet pump solves noise problems."*]

- Did you describe problems from the buyer's point of view? [like *"Labs find it hard to measure the exact amount of additive in formulations"* rather than *"Exact chamber capacity allows increased precision."*]

- Did you describe at least one problem where your product or service can offer a superior solution that differentiates you from competitors?

Thinking about your offering in terms of the problems you can solve gives a useful perspective for planning and asking SPIN® questions.

Having the Right Mind Set

Having the right mind set is crucially important for improving your questioning skills. Asking good questions doesn't come easily for most people, especially when questioning often goes against the strong "telling" habits that come from a product-centered orientation. Many people have told us how unexpectedly difficult they found it to improve their questioning. Here's a typical case study that illustrates how hard it is to change existing habits that have been built up over years. This case comes from a letter sent to us by a reader in Baltimore:

> *I have been selling systems for more than 10 years. When I read* **SPIN® Selling** *I immediately recognized that it was a better way to sell. Without meaning to put down all the research you did, it just seemed so obvious. But it's turned out to be much harder to put into practice than I thought. Two minutes into a meeting and all the questions would go out the window. Instead I'd go back into talking about our products and services. I realized that I was hooked on my old way of selling. It was like a drug. I just couldn't seem to stop myself from talking. I guess the old saying is true that old habits die hard. I'm trying to change but I need help. How do I stop the old habits from getting in the way?*

That's a good question. Old habits *are* powerful. For most of us, the temptation to tell rather to ask is hard to resist. After all, telling has many advantages. For example:

- Telling is *quicker.* It gives the illusion that the discussion is moving faster and therefore is making progress.

- Telling is *easier.* It requires very little planning and even less thought.

- Telling is *safer.* The teller is in the driving seat and has control of the discussion. In contrast, questions put the buyer in the driving seat, which feels a lot riskier.

No wonder most people find it more comfortable to sell by telling rather than by asking. The trouble is that telling is easy but ineffective. Even worse, as the writer from Baltimore put it, it's like a drug. It's hard to kick the telling habit. Many people have tried and have failed. How can you prevent old selling patterns, especially those based on telling, from getting in the way of more effective selling skills?

One useful step in kicking the telling habit is to develop a mind set that encourages questioning. Start by thinking about this T-shirt slogan:

It's more important to understand than to persuade.

Why is this such a profound thought that it deserves a place of honor in the Zen T-shirt Hall of Fame?

A Simple Experiment

Here's a simple experiment that you can try for yourself.

1. Choose someone you know who will be willing to act as your "victim" for this little test.
2. Choose a topic that your victim knows a lot more about than you do, such as a hobby or some area of professional expertise.
3. Take a tape recorder and record a sample of about 10 minutes of conversation between the two of you, where your objective is to *understand* your victim's topic.
4. Next, choose another topic where your objective is to *persuade* your victim of something, such as taking up a hobby that interests you or doing something unusual or new. Record about 10 minutes of this conversation too.
5. Finally, replay and analyze each conversation, using the analysis forms provided. Put a check mark every 15 seconds, depending on who is speaking and whether they are telling or asking questions. Your results will look something like this:

Example

Put one check mark every 15 seconds when …	I'm speaking.	My "victim" is speaking.
The speaker is *telling*	̶H̶H̶ ̶H̶H̶ ̶H̶H̶ ̶H̶H̶ IIII 24	̶H̶H̶ IIII 9
The speaker is *asking*	̶H̶H̶ I 6	I 1

1. Analyze the tape you made when your objective was to *understand.*

Objective = Understanding

Put one check mark every 15 seconds when …	I'm speaking.	My "victim" is speaking.
The speaker is *telling*		
The speaker is *asking*		

From your analysis, answer these questions:
- Who talked more, you or your "victim"?

- Did you *tell* more or *ask* more while your objective was to *understand*?

2. Analyze the tape you made when your objective was to *persuade*.

Objective = Persuading

Put one check mark Every 15 seconds when ...	I'm speaking.	My "victim" is speaking.
The speaker is *telling*		
The speaker is *asking*		

From your analysis, answer these questions:
- Who talked more, you or your "victim"?

- Did you *tell* more or *ask* more while your objective was to *persuade*?

- How does this compare with the tape you made when your objective was to *understand*?

This little experiment generally reveals dramatic results. Even if you think you know the punch line, it's still worth trying for yourself. Most people are amazed to find:

- How much more of the talking they do when they are trying to persuade, compared with when they are trying to understand.

- How they do more telling than they had imagined in their worst nightmares when they are *persuading*.

- How they ask more and they tell less when they are trying to *understand*.

This test demonstrates very effectively how important your mind set can be in altering questioning behavior. If you set out with the objective of understanding your customers rather than persuading them, then you'll find that you'll automatically ask a lot more questions. But, you might wonder, what use is that? Isn't the objective of selling to persuade? If I set out to understand instead of persuade, how will that help me to sell? The answer is one of those great paradoxes that makes psychology so much more interesting than logic. The best way to persuade is not to persuade. Most of the great salespeople we've studied during the last 20 years—and we've had a unique opportunity to study some of the world's best—are much more concerned with understanding than with persuading. They are deeply and insatiably curious about their customers and clients. They have a genuine interest in how their customers see the world. They want to hear about concerns and problems, and they want to understand implications. Persuasion hardly enters into it. As one very successful head of a major consulting company told us:

> *You never persuade clients of anything. Clients persuade themselves. Your function is to understand the issues that matter to your clients. You have to feel their problems just the way they feel them. You have to sit on their side of the table and look at issues from their point of view.*

It would be hard to find a better description of the SPIN® model in action.

6

Focusing on Buyer Needs

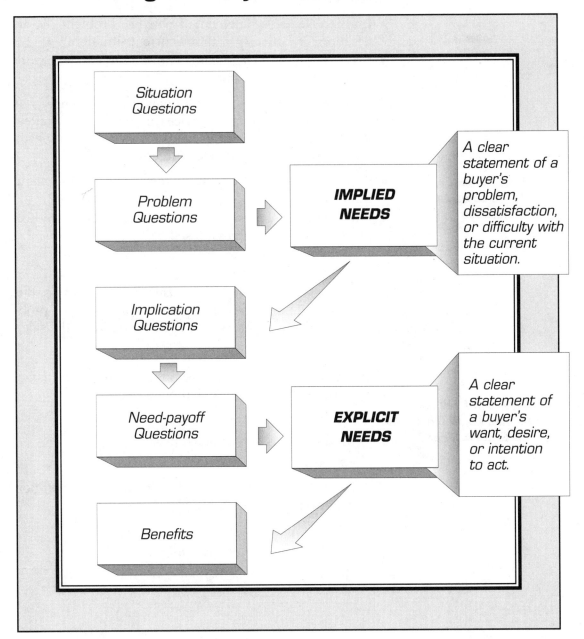

Overview

What's a need?

A *need* is any statement a buyer makes that expresses a concern or want that can be satisfied by the seller. Two kinds of need are key:

- **Implied Need**—a statement of a buyer's problem, dissatisfaction, or difficulty with the current situation.
- **Explicit Need**—a clear statement of a buyer's want, desire, or intention to act.

Customers or clients won't buy unless they have needs or wants that your product or service can satisfy. Huthwaite's research showed that in large sales the two kinds of needs related very differently to sales success:

How do needs relate to sales success?

- Successful sellers uncovered almost exactly the same number of Implied Needs as unsuccessful sellers.
- But successful sellers uncovered over *twice* as many Explicit Needs as unsuccessful sellers.

So, in large sales, effectively developing Explicit Needs is the key to success. But first you have to uncover and understand a buyer's Implied Needs—problems and dissatisfactions—to have the raw material for building the sale.

How can I tell an Implied Need from an Explicit Need?

If the buyer's statement focuses on a problem, dissatisfaction, or difficulty, it's an Implied Need, e.g.:

> *I'm unhappy about service delays.*
> *Breakdowns are a problem when …*
> *I'm worried about interest rates rising for …*

If the buyer expresses a clear want or desire for a solution you can provide, it's an Explicit Need, e.g.:

> *I want faster response time …*
> *I really need 99 percent reliability …*
> *Ideally, interest would be fixed at …*

CHECK YOURSELF—FOCUSING ON BUYER NEEDS

Can you identify which of the following statements are Implied Needs and which are Explicit Needs?

Answers are on the next page.

		Implied or Explicit?
1.	*I'm spending too much on postage each month.*	_____
2.	*I'd like a way to cut my postage costs.*	_____
3.	*I'm looking for help to do a better job forecasting our sales.*	_____
4.	*I'm worried about increasing competition from other contractors.*	_____
5.	*My car has been needing a lot of expensive repairs lately.*	_____
6.	*I need a low-maintenance car.*	_____
7.	*Ideally, if we had the right equipment, we'd be able to reproduce documents in full color.*	_____
8.	*Our patients are complaining about having to wait an hour after they check in at the desk—and some have stopped coming.*	_____
9.	*We really need each team member to be able to send messages automatically to every other team member in the field.*	_____
10.	*Our communication systems aren't as flexible as I'd like.*	_____

1. Implied Need "... spending too much" indicates the buyer's dissatisfaction.

2. Explicit Need "I'd like ..." indicates a desire.

3. Explicit Need "I'm looking for ..." expresses a want or desire.

4. Implied Need "I'm worried ..." indicates a problem or difficulty.

5. Implied Need The buyer is describing dissatisfaction with the existing situation.

6. Explicit Need A clear statement of what the buyer wants.

7. Explicit Need The word "Ideally" indicates a desire for a specific solution.

8. Implied Need "... complaining" and "stopped coming" reflects dissatisfaction.

9. Explicit Need "We really need ..." states clearly what the buyer wants.

10. Implied Need A harder example: "... aren't as flexible as I'd like" describes an undesirable condition.

When in doubt, treat a need as an Implied Need
rather than as an Explicit Need.

How Needs Develop

When potential buyers are sincerely and completely satisfied with the way things are already, they will feel no need to change. What's the first inkling of a need in any of us? We no longer can honestly say we feel 100 percent satisfied with the way things are. And gradually, as our dissatisfaction grows, so does our need for a solution.

What does it mean to be "perfectly satisfied"? That's another way to say that you see no need whatsoever for change. After all, how could a change be better than something that's already perfect? A genuinely satisfied person is entirely happy with the way things are. Such a person feels no need for change and won't buy your products or services. Without needs, there are no sales.

How do needs begin? What is it that turns a perfect situation into one where a sale becomes possible? The first step toward change is that the perfect situation becomes not quite so perfect. The first few days of your brand new car may be perfection, but after a while you notice annoying little dissatisfactions. There's a small rattle somewhere under the hood, a tiny scratch on

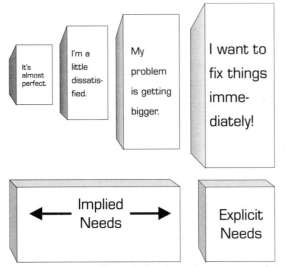

the gleaming paintwork. These are minor irritations—not enough to justify buying a new car—but the process has started. Dissatisfaction, the underlying fuel that powers the development of needs, has crept into the perfect world of your new car. As time goes on your car ages. More things begin to go wrong, it starts to look old and your dissatisfaction grows. In SPIN® terms, you have Implied Needs.

However, as we've seen, although Implied Needs may fuel change, they are not enough to make major sales. After all, a majority of people may be somewhat dissatisfied with their cars, but it's a dissatisfaction that most of them can live with. It's only when their dissatisfaction becomes really severe that it translates into an intention to act. That's when they start to visit showrooms, read consumer reports, and take test drives. Their dissatisfaction has turned into an intention to change. Their Implied Needs, in other words, have become Explicit Needs.

So problems or needs must be developed before a potential customer will buy. That is, a problem must be identified, have urgency, and be translated into an Explicit Need—a clear, strong want or desire for a solution—that you can meet with your product or service.

- In simple sales it takes little skill to develop problems into Explicit Needs.
- In larger, more complex sales it takes considerable skill—and time—to uncover and develop buyer problems (or Implied Needs) into Explicit Needs.

Developing Buyer Needs

Asking the SPIN® questions (covered in detail in Chapters 7–10) is actually a process of shared exploration and understanding focused on the buyer's problems, needs, and wants.

Successful sellers have excellent questioning skills that they use to uncover and develop needs. These skills are the essence of the Investigating Stage discussed in Chapter 4.

The biggest mistake that less successful sellers make in developing needs is to respond to an Implied Need by prematurely introducing their solution. In contrast, successful sellers continue to ask questions. They keep uncovering and developing a buyer's Implied Needs until Explicit Needs emerge.

In fact, in a large or complex sale, jumping too quickly to a solution before needs are fully developed may lose you the sale altogether. Why should that be?

The Value Equation

When someone faces a decision to buy, they have to balance two opposing factors—the seriousness of the problem vs. the cost of the solution.

In a small sale, cost is low enough that even superficial needs can tip the balance. In a larger or more complex sale, the seriousness of the problem has to clearly outweigh the high cost of the solution in order for the customer to buy.

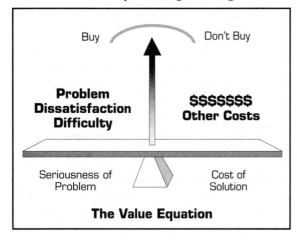

The Value Equation

For example, when pocket calculators were first introduced, they created instant dissatisfaction—an Implied Need—with the bulkiness and inconvenience of large desk calculators. But just as important, the cost of the new calculators was less than one-fifth the cost of the original desk models. So the pocket calculators offered a lot of capabilities for very little money. In other words, they offered very good value. The cost was so low that the Implied Needs were sufficient to tip the balance in favor of purchase. Calculators were a typical small sale, where dissatisfaction (Implied Needs, in other words) was enough to create sales.

The Value Equation and the Larger Sale

The value equation helps you see the larger sale from the buyer's perspective. If the buyer perceives the problem as small and the cost as high, you won't make the sale. *But when the buyer sees the problem as being bigger than the cost of solving it, the person is likely to buy.*

When personal computers first came out, a simple desktop model enabled a professional user to perform an array of financial and other technical analysis, develop and revise proposals and other documents, and perform a host of other functions geared to different industries. Those early PCs offered individuals "mainframe" computer capabilities at a fraction of the old mainframe cost, but the overall cost of changing was still high compared with the cost of the calculator in our earlier example.

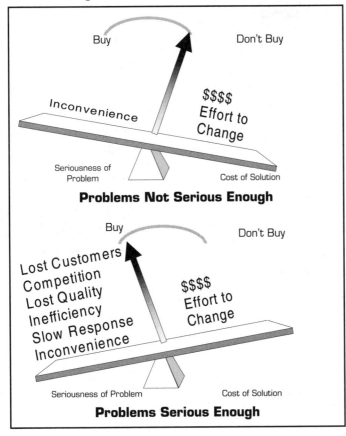

Buy   Don't Buy

Inconvenience $$$$
                                  Effort to
                                  Change

Seriousness of
Problem   Cost of Solution

Problems Not Serious Enough

Buy   Don't Buy

Lost Customers
Competition $$$$
Lost Quality   Effort to
Inefficiency   Change
Slow Response
Inconvenience

Seriousness of Problem   Cost of Solution

Problems Serious Enough

Why did so many companies wait until the middle 1980s before changing their typing pools into word-processing pools, and then wait even longer to buy PCs and network them for professionals to use?

They waited until their dissatisfaction—their perception of the seriousness of their business problems—grew large enough to tip the scale toward a decision to buy. When recessions forced companies to answer questions about how they operated, they came to realize that lost quality, long cycle times, few skilled personnel, and increased competition were causing them to lose customers. They needed to find a way to improve quality, gain flexibility, and use their resources much more efficiently and effectively.

Once their problems were seen as serious enough, buyers looked at purchasing PCs quite differently. What had once seemed like a luxury became a necessary and desirable solution, a way to resolve major business problems. Companies finally bought PCs because they perceived their problems as a *matter of survival.* They began to feel Explicit Needs for change.

Making the Value Equation Work for Your Kind of Sale

Whether you sell computers, flat bed trucks, or architectural design services, first ask yourself "What solution do I offer that is superior to the competition?" The answer becomes an Explicit Need that you want your buyer to express. To achieve this, you must focus your SPIN® questions so that they uncover one or more Implied Needs that you can develop into that Explicit Need you can meet.

Work backwards to the problem!

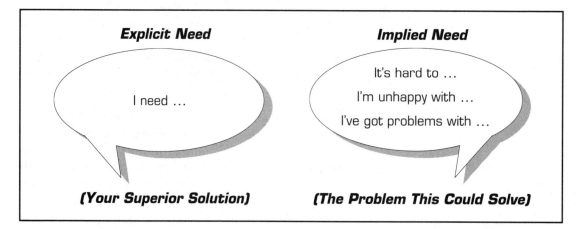

Often the Explicit Need for your solution results from *several* Implied Needs that you develop.

Example

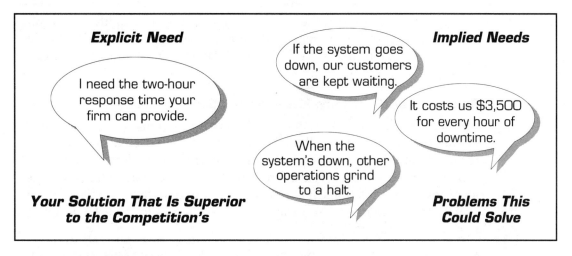

Practice: Working Backwards to Problems

Now it's your turn.

1. Start with the solution you offer that is superior to your competition, that you want your buyer to express as an Explicit Need.

2. List the specific buyer problems that your solution can resolve. Then you can use the SPIN® questions to develop the Explicit Need from these Implied Needs.

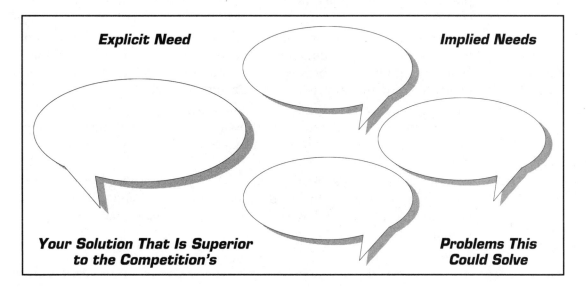

Beyond the Basics—Buyer Needs

This chapter has covered the basics of buyer needs. In real life, developing needs can be a more sophisticated process, especially in large sales. This section and others like it in Chapters 7–11 offer guidelines for handling more complex selling situations.

Strategies for Developing Needs Across Several Functions

In complex sales, the solution may cut across functional areas or traditional lines of responsibility. All the individuals in the affected functions must recognize that they have Explicit Needs before they will buy into your solution. But since each department has different responsibilities and performs different functions, it's unlikely that any two departments will have exactly the same needs. You can use two strategies to develop needs in a large account like this:

- You can use your probing and needs development skills to build each Implied Need so that it becomes Explicit. Even in relatively simple sales, the ability to develop needs in this way is likely to be an important factor in your success.

- You can increase the strength of a need in an account by bringing together smaller needs from several different people or departments. In a large account, successful sellers look at an entire business process or cycle that cuts across functions, then they uncover needs in each department and help buyers understand how the different needs are connected.

A problem may exist in one department that an individual buyer would like to solve, but by itself isn't large enough to justify purchase. So the skilled seller will look for ways to link individual problems into a single overriding one that affects the organization as a whole.

Once you've developed the size and significance of the need beyond a single department's boundaries, showing how your solution can help multiple departments or functions makes the need larger and the cost more acceptable.

And, important as this linking is, the success of this strategy still rests on your ability to develop the needs of each individual you sell to. Before you can link needs, you have to uncover and develop them at the individual level.

Sales May Start with an Explicit Need

In this chapter we've treated the development of needs as if every need you meet when you sell starts off as a minor dissatisfaction and gradually grows into an Explicit Need for change. However, in the real business world, many sales start out with an Explicit Need.

A buyer may tell you at your first meeting, for example, "What I need is speed" and you're slower than the competition. In a case like this, the sale has started with an Explicit Need you can't meet. Successful sellers handle this by taking the buyer back to the Implied Need and developing it in another way, such as:

SELLER   *When you say speed, is that because you have a problem with turnaround time? Couldn't that turnaround time result from the longer reset time that your current equipment requires?*

BUYER   *Well ... I hadn't thought of that.*

SELLER: *So if you had a machine like ours with very short reset times, wouldn't that solve the speed problem?*

BUYER: *Yes, it certainly would.*

In the next four chapters, you'll learn how to use SPIN® questions to uncover problems like these and develop them into Explicit Needs that your products or services can solve.

7

Situation Questions

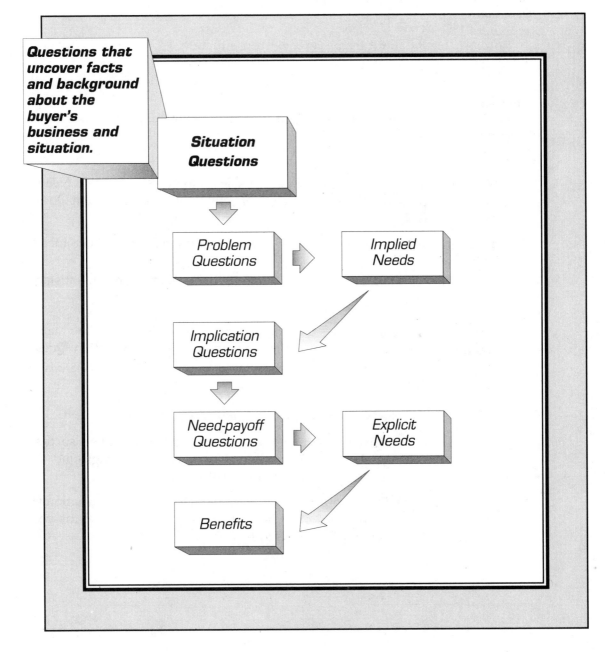

Questions that uncover facts and background about the buyer's business and situation.

Situation Questions

Problem Questions → Implied Needs

Implication Questions

Need-payoff Questions → Explicit Needs

Benefits

Overview

What's a Situation Question?

A *Situation Question* asks for

- Background
- Facts

about the buyer's existing situation.

Why ask Situation Questions?

They help establish a context for uncovering buyer problems.

Since the purpose of questions in larger sales is to uncover Implied Needs and develop them into Explicit Needs, effective sellers ask Situation Questions selectively. They provide:

- Neutral factual information that helps you understand the customer's situation.
- A starting place for deciding which potential problems and dissatisfactions to explore.

Huthwaite's research shows that inexperienced sellers often ask too many Situation Questions or ask them inappropriately. While Situation Questions are an important step in successful selling, asking too many risks losing credibility with the buyer.

The best way to use Situation Questions is to:

So what does that really mean?

- Do your homework before meeting the buyer, so that you're not asking about basic facts and background information that is available elsewhere.
- Focus your Situation Questions to get key information in those areas most likely to uncover buyer problems you can develop into Explicit Needs.

CHECK YOURSELF—SITUATION QUESTIONS

Before we go into more detail on using Situation Questions effectively, let's be sure you're clear about what makes them different from other types of questions. Decide which of the following examples are Situation Questions.

(Yes or No) Situation Question?

1. *What's the average weekly output of this plant?* ☐

2. *How much inventory do you stock on site?* ☐

3. *Do you have problems with backorders on any items?* ☐

4. *Are you happy with your replenishment system?* ☐

5. *Am I right in thinking that you're starting to meet heavy competition from small subcontractors?* ☐

6. *When did you first notice an increase in usage of the billabong machine?* ☐

7. *Are you worried that the increased usage might raise your maintenance costs?* ☐

8. *Has the number of employees who have switched benefit plans met your original projection?* ☐

Answers are on the next page.

SITUATION QUESTIONS—ANSWERS

1. Yes Asking for background information.

2. Yes Seeking to understand how the business operates.

3. No The seller is probing for background problems. So this is a Problem Question, which we'll cover in depth in Chapter 8.

4. No Another Problem Question, asked more indirectly.

5. Yes The seller is checking understanding of the buyer's present market situation. *Note:* This would be a Problem Question if it were asked as "Are you *concerned* about heavy competition from small subcontractors?"

6. Yes The seller is asking for a fact. No problem has yet been uncovered.

7. No This question probes for concerns the buyer may have ("… are you worried?") regarding the increased workload. So this is a Problem Question, but it's a tricky one: If the customer had already stated that the increased workload was a problem, then this would be an Implication Question, asking about the effect of that workload problem on maintenance costs.

8. Yes The seller is asking for a neutral fact. If the answer is that the number fell short of the original projection, then the seller could follow up with a Problem Question to determine if the buyer is dissatisfied with the shortfall.

Using Situation Questions Effectively

After you've done your homework to get basic information about your potential buyer's business, it's important to plan the Situation Questions you'll ask during a face-to-face meeting.

Don't be a prosecutor—be a problem solver

The two main considerations for asking Situation Questions are:

1. **Selecting** the Situation Questions so that you limit the number you'll ask and still obtain the information you need.

2. **Phrasing** your Situation Questions so that they help the buyer see you as a problem solver rather than as a prosecutor.

Let's look at each of these considerations in turn.

Selecting Appropriate Situation Questions

Focusing your Situation Questions prevents you from overloading buyers with questions that might benefit you but bore them—and might even cause you to lose the sale at the very beginning of the Investigating stage.

The best way to avoid asking unnecessary Situation Questions is to:

✔ Be sure each question you ask has a clear purpose.
✔ Ask questions that are related to problems you believe a potential buyer may have that your product or service can resolve.

Later on in this chapter, we'll also review when to ask—and not ask—Situation Questions.

Planning Situation Questions

Is there a practical method for preparing appropriate Situation Questions? Yes.

Remember the *precall planning* you did in earlier chapters to anticipate Implied and Explicit Needs? You can use a similar approach to prepare selected Situation Questions ahead of your customer or client meeting.

Here's how:

1. List some potential problems your product or service could resolve.
2. Determine what factual information you will need before you can effectively investigate those problems.

There can be several different answers in a case like our example on the next page. But what you'll usually find is that:

✔ The *right* Situation Question can lead smoothly and naturally into discussion of the potential problem.
✔ You'll need to ask several Situation Questions before you have enough background to investigate a problem area.

Example

Product/Service: *Automated Storage System*   **Customer:** *V.P. of Logistics*

1. **Potential Buyer Problem** (that you could solve):
   Insufficient storage capacity

2. **Situation Information Needed Before Investigating Problem:**

Situation Questions to Ask	Alternative Source of Information
■ *What kind of storage retrieval system is now used?*	*Warehouse Supervisor*
■ *How many different kinds of goods are stored?*	*Distribution Services brochure*
■ *What's the average retrieval time?*	*???*
■ *How many items are retrieved in a typical day?*	*Warehouse Supervisor?*

Now, try this approach using your own product or service.

Product/Service: _____   **Customer:** _____

1. **Potential Buyer Problem** (that you could solve):

2. **Situation Information Needed Before Investigating Problem:**

Situation Questions to Ask	Alternative Source of Information

Phrasing Your Situation Questions

In certain cases you may get extensive background information before you're positioned to move into problem identification. Since customer interest is generally low during this initial phase, it's important to phrase your questions in a way that will be as acceptable as possible to your customer or client.

Most prospective buyers become irritated if the seller throws a series of blunt and largely unrelated questions at them, such as these questions that a specialty security consultant might ask:

> *What kind of billabongs do you produce here?*
>
> *What kind of chips do they use?*
>
> *How do you store your chips?*
>
> *How old is the local facility?*
>
> *Who's in charge of security for the plant?*
>
> *How many people work on the night shift?*

Such a list of blunt "who, what, how, when, and where" questions can be perceived as a demand for information rather than an attempt to understand the key areas of your buyer's business situation. How can you avoid creating this negative perception?

Linking Your Questions

By *linking* your questions, you can make them flow more smoothly and relate more naturally to your buyer's business concerns:

1. **Linking your questions to buyer statements** can weld a series of questions into a coherent pattern.
2. **Linking your questions to personal observation** can add variety to your questioning and impress the buyer with your alertness.
3. **Links to third-party situations** can boost your credibility, if you can demonstrate understanding and experience with the buyer's business.

Let's look at some examples in the following conversation ...

Example

SELLER   *What kind of billabongs do you produce at this plant?*

BUYER   *We turn out a number of lines, but our principal products are megabillabongs.*

SELLER   *Megabillabongs? What kind of wheezos do they use?* (Links to the buyer's statement.)

BUYER   *We use two kinds of wheezos: general-purpose Cirrus wheezos and Terra wheezos for special 3-D functions.*

SELLER   *I understand that many billabong manufacturers typically keep a three-month supply of Terra wheezos in their component inventory to cover import-related contingencies. Is that about right for your company?* (Links to a third-party situation.)

BUYER   *Yes. In fact, demand for our megabillabongs has increased so much in the last two quarters that we're actually stocking about 20 percent over that.*

SELLER   *During the plant tour, I noticed that there was a large locked "clean room" behind the assembly area. Is that where you store your wheezos?* (Links to the buyer's statement and personal observation.)

BUYER   *Yes. That's where we kept all our environmentally sensitive components until we had to rig some extra storage in Building 2 last month for overflow.*

SELLER   *Building 2 looks older than Building 1. When were they each built?* (Links to the buyer's statement and personal observation.)

BUYER   *Building 2 was the original plant, built in the 1920s. We built Building 1 in the early sixties to better maintain our newer precision equipment.*

SELLER   *That's interesting. With current Terra wheezos prices ranging lately between $60 and $75 each and your increased component stock levels, it sounds like your inventory exposure might be much higher than usual. Is that the case?* (Links to the buyer's statement and third-party information.)

BUYER   *Yes. That's now a worry to Finance as well as to our security manager.* (Buyer has stated an Implied Need that you can develop.)

When to Ask Situation Questions

The most common problem with Situation Questions is not that sellers don't ask them but that they ask them indiscriminately. Focused Situation Questions, thoughtfully phrased and linked to flow naturally, are clearly useful. Knowing *when* to ask Situation Questions, by identifying *high-risk* and *low-risk* areas, is another key to using them effectively:

Low-Risk Areas	*High-Risk Areas*
New customers or clients	Late in selling cycle
Early in selling cycle	Irrelevant business areas
When situations change	Excessive use
	Sensitive areas

Low-Risk Situation Questions

In the following areas, using Situation Questions has low risk and high payoff:

- **New customers or clients**—With new buyers it's necessary to ask a number of Situation Questions, since you don't know much about the operation. Buyers expect to be questioned this way; unless you do so, they will put little faith in your solution. But don't get trapped into staying with easy, safe Situation Questions: It's crucial to move on to what really interests your customers or clients—their problems and how you can solve them.

- **Early in the selling cycle**—Well chosen Situation Questions early in the sale can ease the move into Problem Questions without the seller being perceived as blunt or intrusive. Asking a few focused, neutral, and more indirect Situation Questions about the current operation can set the stage for effectively asking Problem Questions.

- **When situations change**—For current or long-term customers or clients, it's important to stay aware of what's going on in both the internal and external operating environment. By staying informed and in touch, you may uncover opportunities for new business or prevent potential loss of business by taking quick action—for example, when there's an organizational restructuring or a change in the buyer's market.

High-Risk Situation Questions

Because Situation Questions are easy to ask, sellers too often fall back on them when they're inappropriate—as in the following four high-risk areas. *Don't do it!* You'll lose credibility and could lose the sale.

- **Late in the selling cycle**—Either you haven't gathered enough background information (perhaps from not listening closely to the buyer or because of inappropriate earlier questioning), or when you have carried out your sales plan but the buyer has not given you an order or signed a contract and you can't think of anything to say.

- **Irrelevant business areas**—Here the risk is gathering information you cannot use or, worse, uncovering problems you can't solve, since the aim of asking Situation Questions is to lead into areas of dissatisfaction *that you can resolve.* Meetings with potential buyers are much better spent identifying and developing those needs you *can* fulfill.

- **Excessive use**—Some less effective sellers simply ask too many Situation Questions, regardless of whether they can solve the problems that emerge. Excessive use can also test a buyer's patience or create hostility, if you're perceived as that interrogating prosecutor. It's vital to move into the problem areas as soon as you have sufficient background information.

- **Sensitive or potentially sensitive areas**—Examples are asking about the level of sign-off authority your contact has, or questioning an area where there is conflict between your contact's department and another department. Sensitive information is better gathered indirectly and later in the sale when trust has been established.

Beyond the Basics—Situation Questions

You Don't Have to Use the SPIN® Questions in a Rigid Sequence

Successful sellers focus on identifying, understanding, and developing the buyer's problems. So rather than ask lots of Situation Questions early in a sales call, they'll ask them when it makes sense to clarify and explore problems as they actually emerge. For example:

> *You said that employee turnover is a major problem for you. To help me understand this better, could you fill me in on a few facts? For example, how do your compensation rates compare with your competitors'? How often have you revised your benefits package?*

Buyers are much more willing to answer Situation Questions if they believe they're being asked as a means of understanding issues that are important to *them*.

Asking Smart Questions Is Better Than Show and Tell

Some Situation Questions are smarter than others. For example:

> *How are you responding to the recent change in antitrust legislation?* [sounds smarter than] *How long have you been in business?*

Too many people try to show their business knowledge through *telling*, when it's much more credible to *ask*. So, instead of giving a little speech on how much you know about systems integration, you could gain more credibility by asking smart Situation Questions at appropriate points in the investigating stage, for example:

> *How do you integrate satellite configurations into your main platform?*

Gaining Time to Think

Situation Questions are easy to ask, even though they're not very powerful. Sometimes they can provide you with time, while you're considering how to introduce more powerful Problem and Implication Questions.

Experienced sellers usually have a number of Situation Questions they can ask in order to give themselves some breathing room or thinking time to plan Problem Questions or Implication Questions related to issues that are emerging.

SUMMARY CHECK—SITUATION QUESTIONS

1. The purpose of Situation Questions is to:

   True?

   a. Reveal Implied Needs.

   b. Establish a context for uncovering buyer problems.

   c. Explore the implications of buyer problems.

2. Which of these are Situation Questions?

   Situation Question?

   a. *How many trucks operate out of this depot?*

   b. *Does your use of outside contractors create difficulties for you?*

   c. *Do most of your referrals come from other law firms?*

3. Which of these are high-risk for Situation Questions?

   High Risk?

   a. Late in the selling cycle

   b. With new prospective buyers

   c. When the situation has changed

   d. In business areas unrelated to your product or service

4. Your use of Situation Questions can be more effective by:

   True?

   a. Probing every detail of the buyer's operation.

   b. Linking your questions to buyer statements.

   c. Focusing your questions in areas that might reveal problems you could solve for the buyer.

Answers are on the next page.

1. The purpose of Situation Questions is to establish a context for uncovering buyer problems.

2. (a) and (c) are Situation Questions. (b) is a Problem Question.

3. (a) and (d) are high-risk areas for asking Situation Questions.

4. (b) and (c) will make your use of Situation Questions more effective.

8

Problem Questions

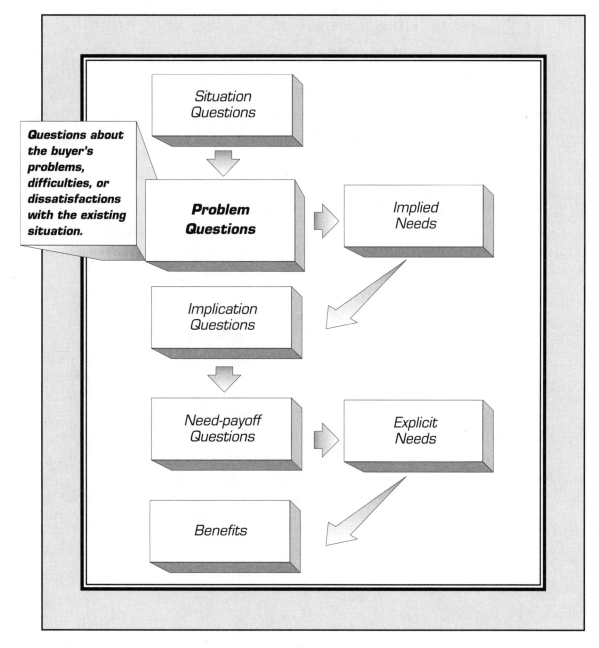

Situation
Questions

**Problem
Questions**

*Questions about
the buyer's
problems,
difficulties, or
dissatisfactions
with the existing
situation.*

Implied
Needs

Implication
Questions

Need-payoff
Questions

Explicit
Needs

Benefits

Overview

What's a Problem Question?

A *Problem Question* asks about people's

- Problems
- Difficulties, or
- Dissatisfactions

with an existing situation.

Why ask Problem Questions?

They help you sell because:

- People buy only if they have *needs.*
- Needs almost always start with a problem or dissatisfaction with the current situation.
- The clearer and more explicit the need, the more likely the buyer is to buy.

To sell effectively, you first have to uncover problems, difficulties, or dissatisfactions—some Implied Needs. That's how Problem Questions help you. Their purpose is to:

- *Reveal* the buyer's Implied Needs.
- *Clarify* the buyer's difficulties and dissatisfactions.
- *Gain shared understanding* of the buyer's problems.

Huthwaite's research shows that Problem Questions are asked more by experienced people and used more in successful calls. And while Problem Questions are linked more strongly to smaller sales, they're still an essential part of effective probing as the sale grows larger.

So what does that really mean?

- You have to uncover problems you can solve, so that you have something useful to offer the customer.
- Problem Questions provide the raw material you need to be able to build the rest of the sale.

CHECK YOURSELF—PROBLEM QUESTIONS

Before you learn more about using Problem Questions effectively, let's be sure you're clear about the difference between Problem Questions and Situation Questions.

	Situation or Problem Question?
1. *How many people do you employ here?*	_____
2. *Is it hard to recruit skilled people?*	_____
3. *Do you have any problem with turnover?*	_____
4. *Have you had any difficulty controlling quality?*	_____
5. *How much has your organization grown during the last year?*	_____
6. *Is any part of the process costing more than you'd like?*	_____

Answers are on the next page.

PROBLEM QUESTIONS—ANSWERS

1. Situation Question   Asking for a fact about the company.

2. Problem Question   Asking about a potential difficulty, which might reveal an Implied Need regarding recruiting skilled people.

3. Problem Question   Asking about another potential problem, which might reveal another Implied Need regarding turnover.

4. Problem Question   Asking about another possible buyer difficulty.

5. Situation Question   Just getting details about the buyer's current situation.

6. Problem Question   A more indirect way of asking the buyer to reveal an area of potential dissatisfaction.

If you had any difficulty with any of these questions, remember our definition of a Problem Question:

A Problem Question asks about the problems, difficulties, or dissatisfactions that buyers have with their existing situations.

Later in this chapter, you'll have an opportunity to practice writing Problem Questions of your own. You'll also have other chances to check your understanding of how to use Problem Questions effectively.

Using Problem Questions Effectively

After you've identified a buyer problem or dissatisfaction by using a Problem Question, it's important to continue revealing and clarifying until you and your buyer share a thorough understanding of the problem or Implied Need.

Follow-up questions that are used to clarify and understand the buyer's Implied Need are also called Problem Questions.

Since you want to engage your buyer in a natural way, it's also important to vary the form of Problem Questions, just as for all the SPIN® questions.

Some useful ways to ask follow-up Problem Questions are *Where? When? Who? How often? What happens if/when?* You can also ask about dissatisfaction or difficulties by asking indirectly, or by using linking phrases, as these examples show:

- *How long does it take for your current service provider to respond when you have a breakdown?*
- *How often does your machine break down?*
- *Where is the breakdown more likely to occur in the process?*
- *Who usually has to deal with the problem?*
- *How satisfied are you with the response time of your current service provider?* (Invites the buyer to express any dissatisfaction with the current response time.)
- *Are there specific parts of the system you think could be improved?* (Invites the buyer to focus on specific problem areas that might be of concern.)
- *You've said that you're basically satisfied with the current response time to fix breakdowns. Since your business has been growing in the past year, are you worried about what will happen now that the workload is increasing?* (Links to a related issue raised by the buyer.)

Could Problem Questions Turn off the Buyer?

Inexperienced people usually find it easier to ask more Situation Questions than Problem Questions, because they're concerned that they'll seem intrusive or negative and might antagonize buyers by asking about dissatisfaction.

But what Huthwaite's research found was that asking too many Situation Questions was more likely to irritate buyers. Why do you think they might react this way?

Why might buyers actually prefer you to ask more Problem Questions?

What Buyers Actually Say

Here are two typical buyer comments about calls that have too many Situation Questions and too few Problem Questions:

> *... boring, and she wasted my time. Maybe the salesperson got something she needed out of the call, but I sure didn't.*

> *The salesperson spent too much time asking for facts he could have found in our annual report. I agreed to the meeting because I thought he might be able to help with our staff turnover concerns, but he never followed up below the surface with any of the problems he brought up.*

In fact, buyers say that asking Problem Questions actually increased their respect for the person asking the questions, because they focus on understanding the buyer's needs.

So, When Asking Problem Questions ...

✔ **Do your homework first.** Ask only a few, well focused Situation Questions that will set the context for asking the Problem Questions you need to ask.

✔ **Do use variety.** Ask Problem Questions directly, indirectly, and through linking phrases.

✔ **Do follow up.** Ask clarifying Problem Questions when your buyer begins to reveal problems, dissatisfactions, or difficulties.

When to ask problem questions and when to avoid them

Knowing WHEN to ask problem questions is important because there are times when these questions may antagonize your buyer.

When to Ask or Not Ask Problem Questions

When to ask or not ask Problem Questions depends on the level of risk involved. In some cases, you will have to ask Problem Questions very carefully or even avoid them until you have established a degree of trust with the customer or client.

There are three high-risk areas where you need to be wary of probing:

- **Sensitive areas**—where the buyer has a high personal or emotional involvement, such as organizational politics, interdepartmental conflict, and public controversies.
- **Recent major decisions**—where probing may be seen as presumptuous or critical, and where your questions might build resistance to using your product or service, even if the buyer's decision was clearly a bad one.
- **Your own product or service**—where the buyer already uses your product or service and asking Problem Questions might create dissatisfaction. (Even if you can offer a superior alternative, be extremely careful to ask Problem Questions only in an area where you can provide additional capability that the competition cannot offer.)

There are also three low-risk areas where Problem Questions should be used freely to uncover and clarify Implied Needs:

- **Early in the selling cycle**—after you've established enough background to set a context and developed enough trust to discuss the buyer's problems.
- **In significant areas**—which might be important to the buyer. The problem has to be important enough so that you can develop the Implied Need into an Explicit Need—a strong desire for a solution.
- **Where you can offer a solution**—since the purpose of asking Problem Questions is to reveal difficulties and dissatisfactions your product or service can resolve.

CHECK YOURSELF—PROBLEM QUESTIONS AND RISK

Now you have a chance to decide when to ask or not ask Problem Questions. Check off which of the following situations would be high-risk and which would be low-risk for you to ask Problem Questions?

	Asking Problem Questions	
	Low Risk	**High Risk**
1. Two weeks ago the buyer installed a new system involving a competitor's product.	☐	☐
2. You have established an Explicit Need for your product and are entering the final stages of the sale.	☐	☐
3. During your first meeting, the buyer tells you they have been using a competitor's services for the past three years.	☐	☐
4. You've established basic facts about the buyer's situation and you're wondering what to do next.	☐	☐
5. The buyer is already making heavy use of your product and you're selling a reorder.	☐	☐
6. The buyer has been having major technical problems with an existing system in an area where your product is strong.	☐	☐

Answers are on the next page.

1. High-risk   The decision is too recent. The buyer is likely to defend the competitor even if real problems exist at this early stage. Asking Problem Questions could create antagonism. After all, nobody likes to admit that they have just made a terrible decision.

2. High-risk   The value of asking Problem Questions is in helping to develop clear and explicit needs. Once you've developed these needs, Problem Questions could raise doubts in the buyer's mind or reopen inappropriate issues. So avoid Problem Questions late in the sale.

3. Low-risk   Asking Problem Questions uncovers areas of dissatisfaction that you can develop into explicit needs. Of course, a buyer who is really happy with a competitor has no problems for you to develop. If so, the sooner you can find that out, the less time you will both waste.

4. Low-risk   This is the ideal time to ask Problem Questions, right after you've established details of the buyer's situation. Having Problem Questions flow naturally from your Situation Questions is best, of course, and that occurs both smoothly and automatically with experienced, successful sellers. Meanwhile, Problem Questions give you the best potential for uncovering Implied Needs.

5. High-risk   If you ask Problem Questions, you may create dissatisfaction with your own product. Only ask Problem Questions if you're offering something different to the buyer.

6. Low-risk   This is the very best area for Problem Questions. The more you can build up the seriousness and size of the problems, the more anxious the buyer will be to buy your solution.

Assessing High Risks in Your Own Cases

Can you think of an existing or potential buyer situation you face that has high risks for asking Problem Questions? Describe it briefly in the first space. Then ask yourself the related questions, and record your answers as you think through each question.

High-Risk Buyer Situation:

---

1. **What is the high-risk area? Why is it high-risk for asking Problem Questions?**

---

2. **Is your relationship with this buyer strong and trusting enough to allow you to ask Problem Questions in the high-risk area?**

Yes ☐   **No** ☐

(If yes, skip to the next page.)

---

3. **In what other, low-risk areas could you ask Problem Questions?**

Putting Problem Questions to Work

Successful use of Problem Questions invites the buyer to state Implied Needs. Remember, Implied Needs provide the raw material for Implication Questions (covered in the next chapter), which are used in large sales to develop the urgency of the buyer's problem and a strong desire for a solution—which your product or service can potentially provide.

Planning your buyer interactions ahead of time is the best way to put all the SPIN® behaviors to work, both to build your skills and achieve successful results. Now it's your turn to practice planning Problem Questions for a prospective buyer of your own.

What Problems Do Your Products or Services Solve?

A good way to start planning Problem Questions is by thinking about the problems your products or services solve for a buyer. Try this exercise first; then move on to the next exercise on the following page.

Problems for Which Our Product or Service Offers a Superior Solution	Kinds of Buyers Who Are Likely to Have This Problem
Example: ■ Our on-line diagnostic service solves the problem of getting critical equipment back into service when a technician isn't available.	*Example:* ■ Small rural hospitals in remote areas ■ Laboratories with night shifts
Try Your Own:	*Try Your Own:*

Now you're ready to begin putting Problem Questions to work with a buyer of your own, zeroing in on the problems you can best solve with your products or services.

Practice Problem Questions with One of
Your Own Buyers

1. Use the planning form on the next page for this exercise. First, select a prospective buyer to practice planning for. Use these criteria to pick a good candidate:
   - You'll be meeting with the prospect in the next week or two.
   - You've done some homework to learn basic facts about the buyer.
   - There's a good chance the prospective buyer has one of the problems you listed in the previous exercise.
   - It will be your first or second face-to-face meeting.
   - There will be little risk involved in trying out a new behavior (Problem Questions) with this buyer.

2. Write the Buyer Name and Meeting Date at the top of the planning form.

3. Identify as many Potential Problem Areas as possible where the buyer could have concerns, difficulties, or dissatisfactions that your product or service could resolve. Write your ideas in the planning form. (Quantity counts!)
   - First list the problems you came up with in the previous exercise that are likely to apply to this prospective customer.
   - Add any other problems that may be unique to this prospective buyer and that your product or service could resolve.

4. Develop a variety of Problem Questions to ask—as many as possible.
   - Write out different variations of Problem Questions.
   - Use direct and indirect Problem Questions.

5. *Use* the Problem Questions you develop!
   - Rehearse your questions ahead of the meeting, if possible, with a colleague.
   - Actually *ask* the buyer the Problem Questions you developed when you meet.

There's nothing wrong with taking your list of Problem Questions into the meeting with you. Very successful salespeople use a question list to prompt themselves during discussions with buyers.

PLAN YOUR OWN PROBLEM QUESTIONS

Customer or Client Name _____ **Meeting Date** _____

Situation (any further facts we need)

Potential Problem Areas (problems that might exist and that we can solve)

Problem Questions to Ask
(to uncover and explore Implied Needs—problems, difficulties, or dissatisfactions)

Beyond the Basics—Problem Questions

Use Follow-up Problem Questions

One important use of Problem Questions is *clarifying* the problems that your buyer identifies. Follow-up Problem Questions clarify specific difficulties or concerns and help you focus your needs development efforts where they'll be more likely to result in a sale.

The purpose of the exercise in Chapter 6, "Working Backward to the Problem," was to show you the importance of looking for the specific problems (Implied Needs) that lead to the Explicit Need you can meet with your superior product or service. Follow-up Problem Questions, such as the following examples, can help you clarify and understand the Implied Needs you should focus on:

> *I want to be sure I'm clear about which kind of [problem] you're having; could you tell me more about [problem]?*
>
> *How often does [problem] happen? Do you have that trouble all the time or only once in a while?*
>
> *It sounds like you're quite concerned about [problem]. Is that the issue that concerns you most?*

The most powerful of all the follow-up Problem Questions you can ask is the magic word—*why?* When a buyer says, *"I'm not satisfied with our current whatsit ...,"* an average seller is impatient to begin talking solutions. But an expert seller asks *"why not?"* or *"why is that a problem?"* The effective seller is careful to clarify the problem *before* asking Implication Questions. Asking *why* can help you:

- Better understand the reasons behind the buyer's dissatisfaction.
- Uncover related problems or effects.

Then you can use what you learn about the problem to ask powerful Implication Questions or focus on a selected problem that your solution can best solve.

Uncover Several Problems before Delving into Implications

Successful sellers uncover several problems before they start asking Implication Questions. Why? A smart seller wants to have several problem avenues to pursue if any individual implication proves to be a dead end. Let's see what happens when a buyer deflects an implication that the seller raises before first uncovering other problems:

SELLER *You mentioned that you've been having a problem with the facing alloy you use. Can you tell me more about that?* [A good follow-up Problem Question]

BUYER *Yes, the bonding often loosens when it goes through the buffer.*

SELLER *So, does that mean you lose production time repairing the bond before final assembly?* [The seller asks an Implication Question, hoping to develop the seriousness of the existing bonding problem.]

BUYER *No, that's not really an issue, because the stamping press resets the bond before final assembly.*

SELLER *Oh ...* [Oops, nowhere to go.]

In the next example, the seller uncovers several problems *before* asking the first Implication Question, so he can develop a different need if the buyer deflects the first one:

SELLER *You mentioned that you've been having a problem with the facing alloy you use. Can you tell me more about that?* [A good follow-up Problem Question]

BUYER *Yes, the bonding often loosens when it goes through the buffer.*

SELLER *Are you having any other difficulties with the facing alloy?*

BUYER *Yes, it loses its tensile strength when it goes through polishing. So we've had to scrap or rework about 10 percent of the pieces. And customer complaints have been increasing.*

SELLER *So does that mean you lose production time repairing the bond before final assembly?* [The seller asks the same Implication Question to develop the seriousness of the existing bonding problem.]

BUYER *No, that's not really an issue, because the stamping press resets the bond before final assembly.*

SELLER *Okay ... could we go back to the scrap problem?* [Or the rework problem or the complaint problem] *Has the 10 percent scrap rate been squeezing your margins?*

Try Seeing the Problem from Different Functional Perspectives

In complex sales, it's important to explore and understand a problem from more than just one perspective. This can build the seriousness of the problem. A good way to start is by asking how your contact thinks the problem might be viewed by someone in another function. For example, *"I can see why that would be a problem for you in manufacturing. How might that concern marketing/product development/finance?"* You may be able to turn the discussion into an invitation to meet with the other decision maker.

1. The purpose of Problem Questions is to:

    a. Reveal Explicit Needs.

    b. Reveal Implied Needs.

    c. Satisfy needs.

True?

Problem Question?

2. Which of these are Problem Questions?

    a. *Do you anticipate any difficulties with output next month?*

    b. *Are there any spare parts in your store?*

    c. *Could this process be improved?*

    d. *How often do you run short of spare parts?*

    e. *How satisfied are you with this process?*

3. When are Problem Questions high-risk and to be used with caution?

    a. Early in the sale
    b. Asking about the buyer's experience with your own products

    c. Asking about recent decisions

    d. In areas important to the buyer's business

High Risk?

4. Problem Questions can be smoothly introduced by:
    a. Asking focused Situation Questions that lead buyers toward potential problem areas.

    b. Only asking Problem Questions late in the sale.

    c. Asking your Problem Questions in a variety of ways.

True?

Answers are on the next page.

1. (b): the purpose of Problem Questions is to reveal Implied Needs.

2. (a), (c), (d), and (e) are Problem Questions.

3. (b) and (c) are high-risk for asking Problem Questions.

4. (a) and (c) are effective ways to introduce Problem Questions smoothly.

9

Implication Questions

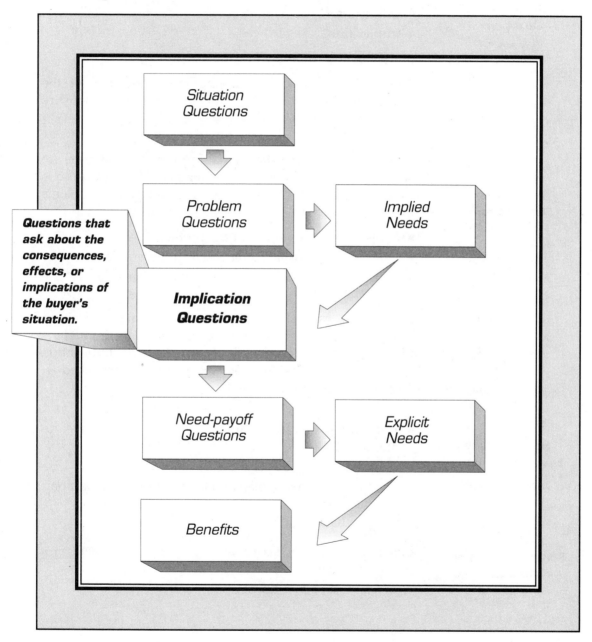

Situation
Questions

Problem
Questions

Implied
Needs

**Questions that
ask about the
consequences,
effects, or
implications of
the buyer's
situation.**

**Implication
Questions**

Need-payoff
Questions

Explicit
Needs

Benefits

Overview

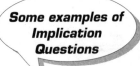

What's an Implication Question?

An *Implication Question* asks about the

- Consequences
- Effects, or
- Implications

of the buyer's situation.

They help you sell by building the seriousness of the buyer's problem so that it becomes large enough to justify action.

Why ask Implication Questions?

Huthwaite's research shows that Implication Questions are strongly related to success in larger sales. Their purpose is to develop the clarity and strength of a buyer's problems by:

- *Focusing on consequences* of the problem.
- *Extending and expanding the effects* of the problem.
- *Linking a problem* to other potential problems.

Implication Questions are especially effective when selling to decision makers—people whose success depends on seeing beyond the immediate problem to underlying effects and possible consequences. Implication Questions help transform problems (Implied Needs) into Explicit Needs—the key buying signal in large sales.

So what does that really mean?

- Implication Questions are a powerful needs development tool.
- They expand the buyer's perception of value.
- They're harder to ask than Situation or Problem Questions.

Some examples of Implication Questions

Could an increase in the value of the components result in a greater risk of theft?

How might that affect your insurance costs?

CHECK YOURSELF—IMPLICATION QUESTIONS

Before you learn more about using Implication Questions effectively, let's be sure you're clear about the difference between Implication and Problem Questions in the following list of examples.

	Problem or Implication Question?
1. *Are you concerned about the increased workload?*	_____
2. *How has the increased workload affected turnover among your support staff?*	_____
3. *Has the shortage of support staff impacted your ability to respond quickly to client calls?*	_____
4. *Are you worried about the quality of work being produced?*	_____
5. *Are you experiencing difficulties recruiting skilled professionals?*	_____
6. *Which category of professionals is hardest to recruit?*	_____
7. *Have these staff problems led you to lose any clients?*	_____
8. *How have you been handling the staff shortage?*	_____

Answers are on the next page.

1. Problem Question   *"Are you concerned ...?"* looks for dissatisfaction.

2. Implication Question   Asking about consequences (*"... has that affected ...?"*) links the increased workload to another problem, staff turnover.

3. Implication Question   The word *impacted* links the problem of staff shortages to another problem, client response time.

4. Problem Question   *"Are you worried ...?"* probes for a different problem.

5. Problem Question   The word *difficulties* asks about yet another problem.

6. Problem Question   *"Which ... is hardest ...?"* follows up on the problem raised in question 5.

7. Implication Question   The phrase *"... led you to lose clients?"* links staff problems to lost clients, which strongly and clearly develops the problem.

8. Problem Question   *"How are you handling ...?"* is a more subtle example. This question still centers around the same problem, neither extending nor linking it to another problem.

Using Implication Questions Effectively

If you missed a few of the previous answers, remember that Implication Questions are harder to prepare than Situation or Problem Questions. But while they are the most challenging of the SPIN® questions to use effectively, Implication Questions are also the most likely to lead to success in larger, more complex sales. Why? Because they are the key to developing problems from Implied Needs into Explicit Needs.

How do Implication Questions help the needs development process? In Chapter 6, you learned that the buyer's problem has to be perceived as bigger than the cost of your solution before a decision to buy will be made. You also learned that an Explicit Need has two components:

The function of Implication Questions is to develop the significance of the problem, so that it becomes clear and strong and the buyer sees it as worth solving.

What Goes into Good Implication Questions?

To ask good Implication Questions, you need:

✔ **Planning**—Implication Questions don't just flow automatically from your mind. Even the most experienced sellers have to think about their Implication Questions ahead of the call.

✔ **Business knowledge**—You've got to understand why a problem might be important to the buyer and what business issues might make it more significant than the buyer realizes.

✔ **Application knowledge**—You must know the kinds of problems your services or products are able to solve, so that you can select the most appropriate Implied Needs to develop.

You Already Know How to Use Implication Questions

Implication Questions are the most challenging of the SPIN® questions used in complex sales, but you already use them in your daily life. Before you try planning for Implication Questions in a business case, it may be helpful to start with a more personal example.

Background

Your friend John is a consultant who commutes in his 10-year-old car from his rural home to his office, about 10 miles away. He travels frequently, using an airport 20 miles away, where he leaves the car in the long-term parking area.

When he's not traveling, John often picks up out-of-town clients who are in town for meetings, shows them the local sights in the evening, or drives to other client meetings in the city or suburbs.

His wife has her own car, but has had to shuttle him to or from the repair shop on occasion and then to or from his office. That has caused them both to have to go to work late or leave early.

You're in John's backyard on Saturday afternoon, when he mentions that he's wondering what to do about his old car. He's worried because the car has been in the repair shop twice lately. He asks you to help him think through the problem.

Your Task

Develop the urgency of the problem by pointing out possible implications.

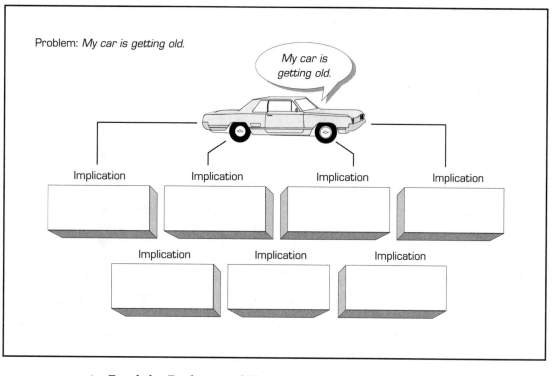

1. Read the Background Description on the previous page.
2. Once you understand the problem, see how many implications you can come up with.
3. Write each implication you come up with in one of the boxes provided above.
4. Draw arrows between the problem and implications, showing the directions you see between cause and effect.
5. Turn to the next page for possible results.

How Implication Questions Work

You might have raised any or all of the following implications:

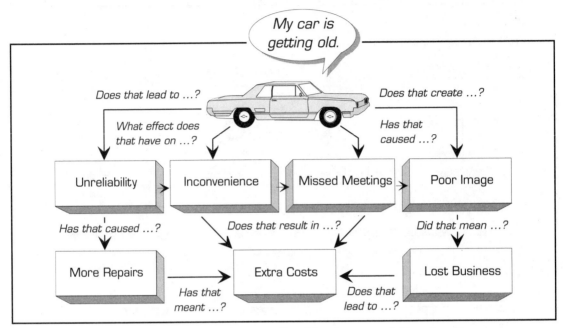

Implication Questions develop a small problem into a much bigger problem.

Did You Notice?

1. One implication often leads to another implication. In our example, reliability problems led to missed meetings, which hurt John's professional image, which led to lost business.

2. Several implications can lead to one overriding problem or issue. This is often the case with cost issues. In our example:
   - Repairs
   - Missed Meetings
   - Poor Image
   - Inconvenience
   - Lost Business
     ... all add up to extra costs.

3. Linking other possible problems or consequences to a given problem clearly increases its significance and urgency to the buyer.

Planning Implication Questions

It's critical to plan Implication Questions in advance of a buyer call. Why? Since they don't automatically come to mind, not planning could cause you to:

- Miss opportunities to ask appropriate Implication Questions when they might have the most impact.
- Cause you to fall back on inappropriate Situation Questions or Problem Questions and thus lose credibility.
- Divert the buyer's attention from problems you *can* solve to problems you *can't* solve.

Remember, the goal of Implication Questions is to build the significance of the problem so that it is clear and strong enough to lead a buyer to feel a strong want or desire for your service or product. So it's important to be clear about the specific problems (or categories of problems if you provide services) the buyer has that you can solve, before planning your Implication Questions.

Four Steps for Planning Effective Implication Questions

Using a client or customer case of your own, try planning some Implication Questions. Don't worry about getting the "right" implications as you practice steps 1–3. At this point, it's more important to try to link each relevant problem with as many possible implications as you can.

1. Make sure you have asked all the Problem Questions necessary for you and the customer or client to uncover and clearly understand the relevant problems—those you can best solve for the buyer.
2. Select the key problems you've already identified that have or that are most likely to have implications you can develop into a need for your products or services.
3. Using the form on the next page:
   - List the selected key buyer problems on the left.
   - List all possible related implications that you think might increase the significance of that problem to the buyer.
4. Prepare some actual Implication Questions to ask the buyer. We'll show you how to phrase effective Implication Questions after you do steps 1–3 on the next page.

Example

Product/Service:	*Product Development Consulting—Project Management Services*
Buyer:	*New V.P. Product Development—(new fiber optic bronchioscope)*
Call Objective:	*Schedule meeting with other key decision makers*

Buyer Problem (that we could solve):	**Implications** (that make problem more urgent):
1. *Current staff already overloaded*	*Quality could be affected.*
	Pressure could lead staff to defect to competition.
	Could lose technology advantage to competition.
2. *Tight schedule to get to market*	*Could miss small window of opportunity.*
	Could lose quality to beat the clock.
	Could lose race to competition.
	Could damage new V.P.'s reputation.

Product/Service:	_____
Buyer:	_____
Call Objective:	_____

Buyer Problem (that we could solve):	**Implications** (that make problem more urgent):
1.	
2.	
3.	

How to Phrase Effective Implication Questions

It's important for your Implication Questions to sound natural and relate appropriately to the buyer's problems. There are three ways to do that:

1. Vary the Way You State Your Implication Questions

Many inexperienced SPIN® sellers get stuck when they're first asking Implication Questions. They ask the buyer to come up with possible implications—by repeatedly asking just one type of general Implication Question such as, *"What are the implications of that problem?"*

To be effective, you need to help the buyer see the seriousness of the problem, by preparing some Implication Questions before your meeting and using a variety of phrases such as:

What effect does that have on ...?

How often does that cause ...?

What does that result in ...?

Does that ever lead to ...?

2. Use a Variety of Different Kinds of Questions

The SPIN® questions are not meant to be used in a rigid sequence. It's appropriate sometimes to follow a Problem Question with a clarifying Situation Question, or an Implication Question with a Problem Question. The key is to ask questions in the sequence that best enables you to establish the context of, uncover, and develop the buyer's problem.

3. Link Your Questions, as you learned to do with Situation Questions in Chapter 7.

- Link your questions to buyer statements.
- Link your questions to personal observation.
- Link your questions to third-party situations.

Now let's look at another sales call that illustrates using these different methods to ask effective, natural Implication Questions.

Example

Peter Roche, from Sound to Go, provides A/V services and equipment to conference centers. The buyer, Julie Crane, manages a conference center.

SELLER *So you manage all the support operations in the conference center?*

BUYER *Yes. Besides managing our audio-visual services, I'm also responsible for housekeeping, catering services, office services, and the related personnel and administrative duties needed to keep our conferences running smoothly.*

SELLER *You said earlier that your conference schedule has been extremely busy for the past year. Has that caused any problems in the A/V area?* [Problem Question linked to buyer's statement]

BUYER *It sure has. In the last three months, I've had to add a second shift of A/V technicians. Our equipment costs have also soared.* [Implied Need]

SELLER *During the tour, I noticed that you had a number of old VCRs and audio cassette players stacked in the corner of your equipment room. Does your A/V staff also do on-site equipment repair?* [Situation Question linked to seller's personal observation]

BUYER *There's usually regular downtime in our conference calendar for repairs. But there's been no downtime for six months and Joe's the only new guy who can fix the old equipment. So now, when we need it, there's no extra equipment we can use.* [Another Implied Need]

SELLER *On the upcoming calendar you showed me, you'll have three months of downtime before you get busy again. If Joe's the only one on second shift doing repairs, how will the rest of the staff be productive during downtime?* [Implication Question linked to seller's personal observation]

BUYER *That'll be a problem. We've got to keep paying the second shift till we get busy again. Before, we used to just pay overtime to the first shift. That saved extra benefit expenses, but we lost good staff as a result.* [Implied Needs]

SELLER *Has your service quality suffered as a result of these staff problems?* [Implication Question linked to buyer's statement]

BUYER *It really has. What I'd really like is a way to have qualified A/V staff on hand in the busy months, and be able to save on payroll and other overhead costs during the slow times.* [Buyer has stated an Explicit Need seller can meet]

Implication Questions and the Complex Sale

In the complex sale you will usually be making a series of fact-gathering calls. Once you have a clear understanding of the organization and operation, you'll have time in advance of the actual buyer discussion to pore over the problem areas you've uncovered and consider the potential linkages between them.

Planning ahead like this will help you to link issues in subsequent discussions with your buyer.

Knowing the issues thoroughly will also help you prepare a variety of Implication Questions. That way you'll be prepared if additional consequences or related issues emerge during the buyer discussion that might require you to think on your feet.

When to Ask Implication Questions and When to Avoid Them

Ask Implication Questions after Problem Questions, but before introducing your solution.

One of the most frequent and dangerous mistakes a seller can make is to introduce a solution before the Explicit Need has been fully developed. When the customer agrees that a problem exists, it's tempting to jump in with solutions. After all, the buyer's got a problem and you're there to provide answers. *Don't do it!*

Instead, build a bridge to your solution first. Use Implication Questions that develop and extend the importance of the problem, so that when you do propose a solution, your buyer's interest will be high.

Low-Risk Implication Questions

There are three low-risk areas where Implication Questions are especially valuable for developing and extending problems:

> **When problems are significant**
> **When problems are unclear**
> **When problems require redefinition**

- **When problems are significant.** A buyer will readily tell you about issues like costs, wasted time, inconvenience, lost opportunities. Implication Questions also have high payoffs when the problem is complex or has a chain of ramifications.

  Ben Franklin, who would have been a very effective seller, wrote a classic verse that illustrates how implications in a chain of ramifications can be used to develop and extend a problem.

- **When problems are unclear.** You can help bring them into sharper focus by asking Implication Questions. Helping your buyer think through tough problems can also strengthen trust and build a better working relationship.

- **When problems require definition.** Sometimes it seems you can only offer a partial solution to the problem as it's described. But if the buyer can be helped to think about it from another perspective, redefining the problem, your solution might fit better. An effective use of Implication Questions here can build the elements of the problems that your solution answers most strongly, increasing your chances of making a sale.

High-Risk Implication Questions

The three occasions when Implication Questions should not be used or used with care are:

> **Too early in the call**
> **With implications you can't solve**
> **In sensitive areas**

- **Too early in the call.** It's dangerous to ask Implication Questions before you have established a solid understanding of the buyer's situation. Avoid creating mistrust or provoking buyer resistance by too abruptly probing for implications. It's best to warm the call up with Situation Questions before asking about problems and implications.

- **With implications you can't solve.** Save your Implication Questions for building the significance of problems you *can* solve.

- **In sensitive areas.** It's always risky to delve into implications in sensitive areas such as organizational politics, personal issues, or decisions that the buyer has recently made.

Practice Your Own Implication Questions

1. Select one of the implications you developed earlier in this chapter for one of your buyers.
2. List the implication you selected in the space provided below.
3. Prepare at least three variations of Implication Questions based on the single implication you selected, and list them in the spaces provided.

Example

Implication: *The tight schedule means you could lose quality to beat the clock.*
Implication Questions:

> *What impact could the tight schedule have on the quality of the bronchioscope?*
>
> *Quality often suffers when you're racing the clock. Do you feel that's a risk here?*
>
> *What are the down sides from such a tight schedule in terms of quality?*
>
> *Can you talk about any risks you see of quality being affected by the tight schedule?*
>
> *If you've only got three months, are you going to be able to keep quality the same?*

Your Implication

Your Implication Questions

Beyond the Basics—Implication Questions

Problem Questions focus inside the problem, while Implication Questions focus outside the problem:

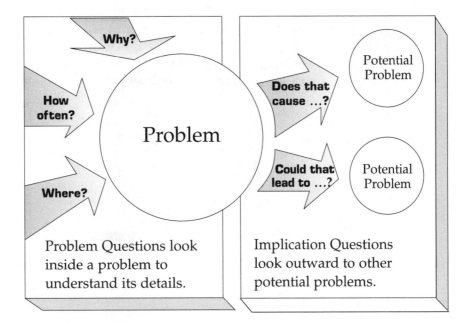

Problem Questions look inside a problem to understand its details.

Implication Questions look outward to other potential problems.

Ask Implication Questions as Much to Understand as to Persuade

Implication Questions increase pain by extending the seriousness of the problems. A fundamental principle of consulting, which applies equally to selling, is that good consulting keeps the client in moderate pain but never allows that pain to become excessive. Asking too many Implication Questions or working too hard to build pain can be counterproductive. Remember that your buyer can tolerate only a certain amount of discomfort. Don't go beyond a reasonable level.

Inexperienced people, when first working with Implication Questions, feel they've succeeded only when they've increased their buyer's pain level. Very successful sellers, however, will ask Implication Questions more to understand than to persuade. So if they ask, *"What effect does this have on costs?"* and the buyer says, *"None. That doesn't affect costs because we have so much spare capacity,"* a good seller will be content. Experienced sellers find it's just as important to learn that the implications don't in fact exist where they anticipated them. This way they can focus on the areas that matter most to their buyers.

Implication Questions Can Link Various Departmental Problems into One Serious Company Problem

When you're dealing with multiple buyers or a buying committee in a company, Implication Questions become a vital means of uncovering common ground for a shared sense of urgency around a multifaceted problem. Similarly, Implication Questions can link their internal problems with external customer problems that could translate into loss or potential loss of income for the entire company. When a small problem grows until it results in lost income, how can that company afford *not* to buy the solution?

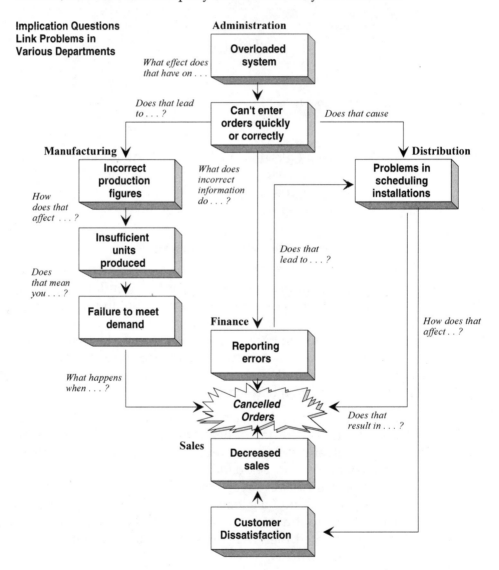

Implication Questions Link Problems in Various Departments

Implication Questions—Summary Check

Check your understanding of the use of Implication Questions by answering the following questions.

1. The purpose of Implication Questions is to:

   True?

   a. Identify buyer problems.

   b. Demonstrate the implications of your service or product.

   c. Develop Implied Needs so that they become Explicit.

2. Which of these is/are Implication Questions?

   Implication Question?

   a. *Do these breakdowns lead to production difficulties?*

   b. *Have you got more than seven trucks on-site?*

   c. *And if your staff shortage causes filings to be delayed, how much longer does it take to close those cases?*

3. Which of these create(s) high risk for Implication Questions?

   High Risk?

   a. When the buyer is unclear about the importance of a problem

   b. Very early in the sale

   c. When you're unable to solve the buyer's problem in any way

4. The time to ask Implication Questions is:

   Choose One

   a. After you demonstrate the capability of your solution.
   b. After you investigate the buyer's solution but before you ask about problems.
   c. After a buyer describes a problem but before you introduce your solution.

Answers are on the next page.

SUMMARY CHECK—ANSWERS

1. The purpose of Implication Questions is to develop Implied Needs so that they become Explicit Needs.

2. (a) and (c) are Implication Questions. In (a) the breakdown is the problem—production difficulties are a consequence (implication) of the problem. In (c), the inability to make the filings on time is the problem—delay in closing cases is a possible implication.

3. (b) and (c) are high-risk for asking Implication Questions.

4. (c) is correct. The time to ask Implication Questions is after a buyer describes the problem but before you introduce your solution.

10

Need-payoff Questions

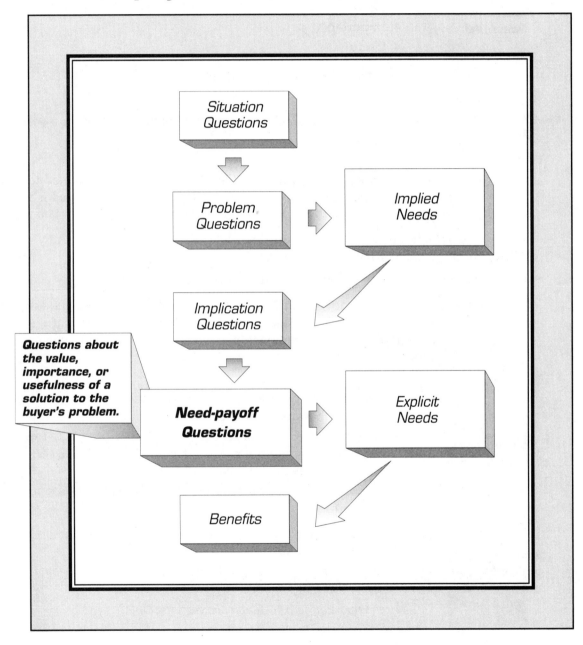

Situation
Questions

Problem
Questions

Implied
Needs

Implication
Questions

**Questions about
the value,
importance, or
usefulness of a
solution to the
buyer's problem.**

**Need-payoff
Questions**

Explicit
Needs

Benefits

Overview

What's a Need-payoff Question?

A *Need-payoff Question* asks about the

- Value
- Importance, or
- Usefulness

of the *solution.*

Why ask Need-payoff Questions?

They help you sell by increasing the attractiveness of a solution.

Need-payoff Questions, like Implication Questions, are strongly related to success in larger sales. Their purpose is to develop the buyer's desire for a solution by:

- **Focusing on the payoff of a solution** instead of the problem.
- **Probing for Explicit Needs.**
- **Getting the buyer to tell you the benefits** of the solution.

Huthwaite's research shows that Need-payoff Questions increase the acceptability of your solution and are particularly effective in sales that depend on maintaining a good relationship, such as sales to existing clients or customers.

So what does that really mean?

- Need-payoff Questions are positive, helpful, and constructive, because they focus on the solution.
- They reduce objections, because they cause buyers to explain how your solutions can help and, in doing so, convince themselves of the value of your solutions.
- They move the discussion forward towards action and commitment.

Some examples of Need-payoff Questions

How much of a saving would this mean?

What other tasks would the streamlined process enable you to complete that you can't do now?

How important is it to double the response time?

CHECK YOURSELF—NEED-PAYOFF QUESTIONS

Before you learn more about using Need-payoff Questions, see if you're clear about the difference between Need-payoff Questions and the other SPIN® questions.

	Need-payoff Question?
1. *How much would you save annually if we could eliminate your seasonal overtime costs?*	_____
2. *How much has tardiness increased because of the relocation?*	_____
3. *Would it be useful to have modules you can mix and match and reconfigure as your needs continue to change?*	_____
4. *If we could shorten your order processing cycle by two days, how many more billabongs could you ship each week?*	_____
5. *Are you worried about the unreliability of the current system?*	_____
6 *Would it help if I could show you a way to overcome the contamination problem?*	_____
7. *Could the new system also help you maintain better stock control?*	_____
8. *Has the staff shortage caused you to miss important calls?*	_____

Answers are on the next page.

1. Yes   The question is about the value of a solution to the overtime problem.

2. No   This is an Implication Question, developing the seriousness of the problem, not the solution.

3. Yes   The question asks the buyer about the usefulness of the proposed solution.

4. Yes   The solution being explored involves saving two processing days. The worth or importance of the solution is developed in terms of output.

5. No   This is a Problem Question, because it asks about buyer concerns, dissatisfactions or difficulties.

6. Yes   This is clearly a question about the importance or value of a solution. As we'll see later, many sellers make the mistake of asking *"If I could show you a way …"* questions too early in the call.

7. Yes   The solution (our new system) is being developed into other payoff areas.

8. No   This is an Implication Question, since it extends the staff shortage problem to possible missed calls.

Using Need-Payoff Questions Effectively

Need-payoff Questions are fundamentally different from all the other SPIN® questions. They aren't easy questions to ask, and you have to ask them at the right point in the sale. But they are one of the most powerful types of question and they can help you get results.

How do Need-payoff Questions help achieve sales success? In Chapter 9 you learned that an Implication Question develops one of the two components of an Explicit Need: It builds the buyer's *problem* so that it is strong and clear. A Need-payoff Question addresses the other component of an Explicit Need: *the desire for a solution.*

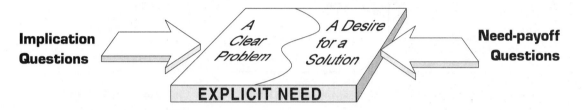

How Need-payoff Questions Help You Sell

Understanding the different functions of Need-payoff Questions will make them easier to ask and will be helpful in selling more effectively. The three functions of Need-payoff Questions are to:

✔ **Identify Explicit Needs**—One function of Need-payoff Questions is to uncover whether or not an Explicit Need exists; for example, *"Do you need a faster machine?"* or *"Would it help you to have a reliable source of supply?"* This is what most people mean by Need-payoff Question. But the other two functions, less often used, can have even more influence on the buyer.

✔ **Clarify Explicit Needs**—These Need-payoff Questions get the client or customer to explain the importance of the need in detail by asking such things as *"Why is that important to you?"* or *"Could you tell me more about your need for flexibility?"* or *"Do you want faster turnaround to save costs or to better utilize your other equipment?"* If it's a need you can solve, this kind of question gets the buyer to tell *you* the Benefits. And the buyer's acceptance is key to a successful sale.

✔ **Extend Explicit Needs**—These Need-payoff Questions invite the buyer to specify additional payoffs by asking, for example, *"Is there any other way this would help you?"* or *"Besides adding useful space, would the design enhance your image?"* or *"What other benefits could you foresee from using this solution?"* Their responses can help your solution offer extra value to the buyer.

Try Out the ICE Model

The *ICE* (*Identify, Clarify, Extend*) model puts these three functions together to enable you to plan different levels of Need-payoff Questions. Here's how it works:

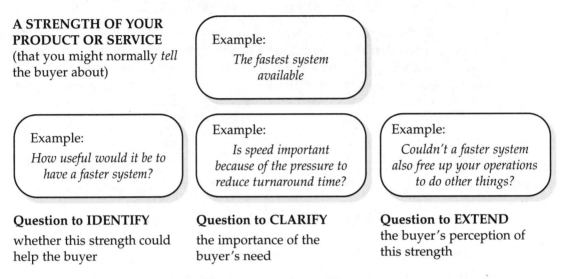

A STRENGTH OF YOUR PRODUCT OR SERVICE
(that you might normally *tell* the buyer about)

Example:

The fastest system available

Example:

How useful would it be to have a faster system?

Example:

Is speed important because of the pressure to reduce turnaround time?

Example:

Couldn't a faster system also free up your operations to do other things?

Question to IDENTIFY
whether this strength could help the buyer

Question to CLARIFY
the importance of the buyer's need

Question to EXTEND
the buyer's perception of this strength

Now try this exercise with a case of your own:

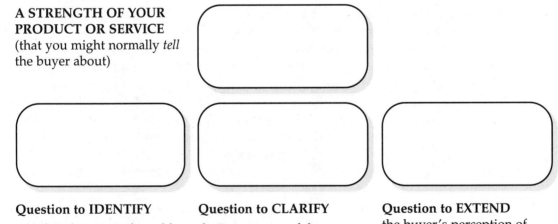

A STRENGTH OF YOUR PRODUCT OR SERVICE
(that you might normally *tell* the buyer about)

Question to IDENTIFY
whether this strength could help the buyer

Question to CLARIFY
the importance of the buyer's need

Question to EXTEND
the buyer's perception of this strength

How NOT to Ask Need-payoff Questions

The purpose of Need-payoff Questions is to clarify and develop the buyer's perception of payoff from your product or service and thus develop a clear explicit desire for your solution.

But whether *you* believe your solution has value for the buyer is irrelevant. Unless the buyer believes it, you won't make a sale. And unless your buyer is willing to *do* something—to take action—you still won't make a sale.

We've mentioned already that one of the biggest mistakes sellers make is introducing their solution before they've built the seriousness of the buyer's problem. Because Need-payoff Questions focus on solutions, they can have a negative effect if they're used too early in the sale. And if introduced too early in the discussion, they can make the potential buyer feel confused or manipulated.

Helping Buyers Understand the Payoff of Your Solution

Since you know the capabilities of your product or service, it's generally much easier for you to see the payoff than it is for the buyer. You have to help by *developing* the buyer's desire for a solution. Need-payoff Questions enable you to establish the range of payoff areas and their importance to the buyer. There are two ways to do this, as these examples illustrate:

Question 1

Ms. Buyer, if I could help you save time on this operation, would that be useful to you?

Ms. Buyer, if I could help you save time on this operation, what would that enable you to do that you can't do now?

Question 2

Which of these two questions is more likely to have the buyer *actively specify payoffs*?

The answer is Question 2. Question 1 allows the buyer to passively accept payoffs without thinking about the solution. Question 2, however, asks they buyer to actively specify the payoffs from solving the problem—particular things this buyer would be able to do as a result of the solution that can't be done now.

Such an active thinking process often extends a buyer's Explicit Need into new payoff areas. But it has an even more important function:

> *Because they've specified the payoffs, buyers will be more committed to your solution and feel more ownership of it.*

Need-payoff Questions and the Complex Sale

In a simple sale there's usually a straightforward relationship between your product or service and the problem it solves. The solution may even fit the problem exactly. So, for example, a person worried about fire risks for important company papers has a problem that might be solved perfectly by purchasing a fireproof filing cabinet.

There Are No Perfect Solutions in a Complex Sale

But as the sale grows more complex, the fit between problem and solution becomes less straightforward. Problems in the complex sale may have many parts, and the solution you offer will deal with some of these parts better than others. A problem such as low productivity, for example, could be caused by dozens of factors. When you present your solution, you run the risk of having the buyer focus on the areas you *don't solve* rather than the ones you do solve. In that case, the buyer might challenge your whole solution, as this example shows:

SELLER *So your main problem is a high reject rate on the material you use for technical tests. Our new material is so easy to use that your technicians' reject rate would be reduced by 20 percent.*

BUYER *No. Wait a minute. It's not only the test material that creates the reject rate. There are a lot of other factors, like processor temperature and developer oxidation. So don't give me all that stuff about easy-to-use material.*

What's happening here? The buyer is raising objections because the seller's solution only deals with one facet of a complicated problem. By making claims for the product, the seller prompts the buyer to think about some of the other facets and reject the point the seller is trying to make.

In a complex sale, the problems you're trying to solve will almost always have many facets. It's unlikely that you or any of your competitors will be able to provide a perfect solution that can resolve every facet of a complex problem. Nor does the buyer really expect your solution to be perfect.

Sophisticated business people look for the ability to deal with the most important elements of the problem at a reasonable cost. And because vendors rarely have a perfect solution, it's dangerous for you to point out how well you can solve a problem. By doing so you invite the buyer to focus on the elements you *don't* solve and to raise objections.

How can you gain the customer's acceptance that your solution has value, even though it may not solve every facet of the problem? This is where Need-payoff Questions can be very helpful.

Need-Payoff Questions Reduce Objections

Need-payoff Questions get the buyer to explain which parts of the problem your solution *can* solve. When the *buyer* tells you the ways your solution can help, then you don't invite objections.

Using Need-payoff Questions makes your solution more acceptable to the buyer, as the next example shows:

SELLER *So your main problem is a high reject rate on the material you use for technical tests. And from what you've said, you'd be interested in anything that could reduce that reject rate.*

BUYER *Oh yes. It's a big problem and we've got to take action.*

SELLER *Suppose you had a material that was easier for your technicians to use. Would that help?*

BUYER *It would be one factor. Remember, there're a lot of other factors, like processor temperature and developer oxidation.*

SELLER *Yes, I understand that there are several factors and, as you say, an easier material is one of them. Would you explain how having an easier material would help you?*

BUYER *Well ... it would certainly cut some of the rejects we're getting at the exposure stage.*

SELLER *And would that be worth doing?*

BUYER *Probably. I don't know exactly how much is lost there, but it might be enough to make some difference.*

SELLER *Is there any other way using an easier material could help?*

BUYER *Those neat cassettes of yours don't require an experienced technician to set them up. Maybe that would help ... yes ... if we had a material that was easy enough for an assistant to set up, then the technician could spend more time on the processing stages, which could make a big impact on those processor problems we've been having. Hey, I like it ...*

In this example, the seller's use of Need-payoff Questions has enabled the *buyer* to explain the payoff and, as a result, to find the solution more acceptable.

Planning Need-payoff Questions

To plan for asking Need-payoff Questions, think about potential payoffs of your solution from the buyer's point of view, based on the relevant problems you've explored.

Be sure you identify any problems that still need to be clarified and developed by asking Situation, Problem, and especially Implication Questions, so that the buyer will be receptive to this payoff.

Example

Product/Service: *A/V services and equipment*

---

1. **Potential Area of Buyer Payoff:**

Decrease A/V costs 20 percent, while improving response time and quality, regardless of seasonal demand fluctuations.

2. **Problems You Could Resolve That Need to Be Developed Before Buyer Fully Recognizes Payoff:**

- *Costs of second shift A/V staff—especially during off-season (idle time)*
- *Complaints of poor A/V response times during busy season*
- *Possible effects on overall service quality due to lack of equipment knowledge*
- *Possible impacts of busy manager spending so much time handling A/V staffing problems*

Planning Need-payoff Questions

Now try this method with a case of your own.

1. Write down a potential payoff that the buyer could get from your solution.

2. List any problems you may need to develop by using the other SPIN® questions, especially Implication Questions, so the buyer will feel strongly enough to want a solution.

Product/Service:

1. **Potential Area of Buyer Payoff:**

2. **Problems You Could Resolve That Need to Be Developed Before Buyer Fully Recognizes Payoff:**

Having done this exercise, you probably found that you need to uncover and develop several problems before a buyer will fully realize the potential payoffs from your solution.

Later in this chapter, you'll also have a chance to practice the next step: preparing the actual Need-payoff Questions to ask your buyer.

When to Ask Need-payoff Questions and
When to Avoid Them

Few sellers ask Need-payoff Questions at the optimal point in the sale. If you ask them too soon, such as right at the start of the call, then the buyer's lack of clarity about problems prevents you from effectively developing a strong desire for a solution.

At the other end of the scale, many sellers wait until too late to ask Need-payoff Questions. They describe their solutions before they generate an appetite for what they can offer. As we've seen, this very frequently provokes objections from the buyer.

The best time to ask Need-payoff Questions is:

✔ **Before** describing your solution, *and*
✔ **After** developing the seriousness of the buyer's problem by using Implication Questions.

Although the research has clearly shown that more Need-payoff Questions are asked in successful sales, the average seller uses fewer than two Need-payoff Questions in a typical call. Yet when used at the right point, Need-payoff Questions increase the chance of making a sale.

Low-Risk Need-payoff Questions

The are two low-risk areas where Need-payoff Questions are especially valuable for increasing a buyer's desire for your solution:

- **When the solution has payoffs in other areas**—If there are potential spinoff benefits as a result of your solution, Need-payoff Questions are especially powerful in helping you sell. Asking a Need-payoff Question like *"What could you do with the extra time our solution would save you?"* or *"Are there other ways this solution would improve ...?"* can get the buyer thinking of additional benefits you can develop, especially given the complexity of many buyer situations.

- **When the buyer has to justify the decision**—Even a buyer with purchasing authority may need to justify the purchase to management, a board, or others. The more you use Need-payoff Questions to clarify and develop the buyer's understanding and ownership of the potential benefits of your solution, the easier it will be for the buyer to communicate about them to others in their organization. By answering your Need-payoff Questions, the buyer practices explaining how your solution will help.

High-Risk Need-payoff Questions

Other areas are high-risk for asking Need-payoff Questions. Be cautious about using them:

- **Too early in the call**—Your Need-payoff Questions won't have any real effect unless and until the buyer has recognized and clarified a problem. Asked before this point, they may even antagonize buyers into denying the existence of genuine problems and needs.

- **When the buyer's need is subjective**—Sometimes a buyer just likes your product or is prepared to purchase your services when few of the objective facts about problems and their implications directly support a decision to buy. In such a case it's important to help the buyer think through the business reasons for buying your solution. First, be sure to identify and develop the buyer's needs by asking Problem and Implication Questions. Then, selectively ask your Need-payoff Questions to develop and extend solutions that meet the buyer's identified needs.

How to Phrase Effective Need-payoff Questions

Once you've used Implication Questions to fully develop the relevant problems on your list, you'll find it easier to ask Need-payoff Questions smoothly and naturally. Using the following methods will help you prepare effective Need-payoff Questions:

✔ **Use linking phrases**—Link your questions to buyer statements or responses.

> *If there were a way for you to get out of that day-to-day payroll administration, how would it help you cover the other areas you manage?*

> *You mentioned that you have to replace a lot of heat-damaged customized transparencies. At $50 each, wouldn't it be worth paying a higher one-time cost for a projector that would increase their working life?*

✔ **Use variety**—Be clear and specific, and avoid repetition of the same phrase, such as:

> *How would this help you save time?*

> *How would this help you reduce costs?*

> *How would this help you speed up response times?*

Instead, you could ask, e.g.,

> *How could you use the time you'd save?*

> *What budget relief would you get in other areas if our volume discount saved you over 15 percent?*

> *Would it speed response time if you had people who were fully trained in repairing both current and older equipment?*

✔ **Get the buyer to actively specify payoffs**—Wherever possible, use Need-payoff Questions that ask your *buyers* to actively specify the payoffs that are important to *them*, e.g.,

Passive Acknowledgment:

> *Wouldn't it save time?*

Buyer Actively Specifies Payoffs:

> *What important projects could you work on if you didn't have to spend so much time on billing problems?*

Practice Your Own Need-payoff Questions

1. List the potential payoff area you identified in the earlier exercise, Planning Need-payoff Questions.
2. Prepare 3–5 variations of Need-payoff Questions based on that one potential payoff, listing them in the spaces provided below.

Example

Payoff:

Decrease A/V staffing costs 20 percent, while improving response time and equipment quality, regardless of seasonal demand fluctuations.

Need-payoff Questions:

If you could reduce your annual A/V staffing costs by 20 percent, what would you do with the savings?

How would your other management responsibilities benefit if you didn't have to spend time dealing with A/V staffing problems?

Are response time and equipment quality equally important to you?

How valuable would it be for you to be able to reduce A/V staffing costs while actually improving response time?

If seasonal demands didn't affect A/V staffing levels, how would that help you?

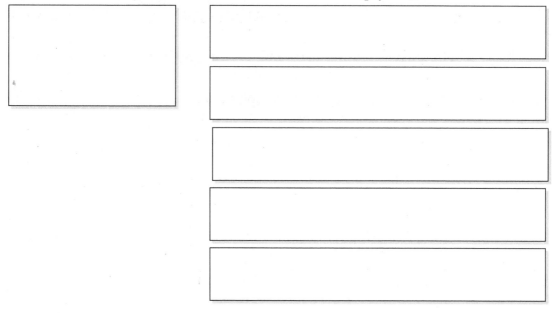

Your Potential Payoff

Your Need-payoff Questions

Beyond the Basics—Need-payoff Questions

Need-payoff Questions Help Rehearse Internal Sponsors to Sell for You

As the size of a sale grows, more people become involved in the decision. Your success depends not just on how well you sell but how well people in the targeted organization sell to each other. Successful sellers help internal users and influencers sell a solution on their behalf.

When opportunities are limited for you to meet with the ultimate decision maker (or decision-making team), one of the best ways to sell is rehearsing the internal people who will be selling *for* you. The better prepared your internal sponsors are, the easier it will be for them to sell your solution to others.

But what *is* the best way to rehearse an internal sponsor? Need-payoff Questions have a special use here. By getting the *buyer* to describe Benefits, Need-payoff Questions accomplish several things:

- **The buyer's attention is focused on how the solution will help, not on product details.** Need-payoff Questions engage your sponsors in identifying exactly how the solution you're proposing will meet their company's needs. Discussing these Benefits with others in the business who share the same needs is the most effective way that they can sell for you.
- **The buyer explains the Benefits to the seller, not vice versa.** It's a much better rehearsal for buyers to actively describe Benefits in their own words than to listen passively while you do it. This way the buyer will remember the Benefits you offer.
- **The buyer's enthusiasm and confidence in your solution are increased.** Those qualities will sell for you when you're not present.

You'll find more details and examples of using Need-payoff Questions to rehearse your sponsor in *SPIN® Selling*, pages 85–88.

NEED-PAYOFF QUESTIONS—SUMMARY CHECK

Check your understanding of the use of Need-payoff Questions by answering the following questions.

1. The purpose of Need-payoff Questions is to:

   True?

   a. Develop and extend a buyer's problems.

   b. Increase a buyer's desire for a solution to a problem.

   c. Expose problems that your product or service can solve.

2. Which of these are Need-payoff Questions?

   **Need-Payoff
   Question?**

   a. *What would it be worth if you could double output in these areas?*

   b. *What other ways could this help you?*

   c. *What impacts does this problem have on production?*

3. The time to ask Need-payoff Questions is:

   Check One

   a. Early in the call before you've uncovered a buyer's problem.

   b. After you've demonstrated the capabilities of your product or service.

   c. After you've developed a buyer's problem but before you've introduced your solution.

4. Which of these would cause a buyer to *actively specify payoffs*?

   Check One

   a. *Would you be interested in increasing your output?*

   b. *What would a 10 percent increase in output mean to your profitability?*

   c. *How would the improved cash flow help you?*

Answers are on the next page.

1. (b): The purpose of Need-payoff Questions is to increase a buyer's desire for a solution to a problem.

2. (a) and (b): The exception is (c)—an Implication Question that develops a problem, not a solution. (See Chapter 9.)

3. (c): The time to ask Need-payoff Questions is after you've developed a buyer's problems but before you introduce your solution.

4. (b) and (c): These questions ask buyers to specify the payoffs of the solution in their own terms.

11

Demonstrating Capability

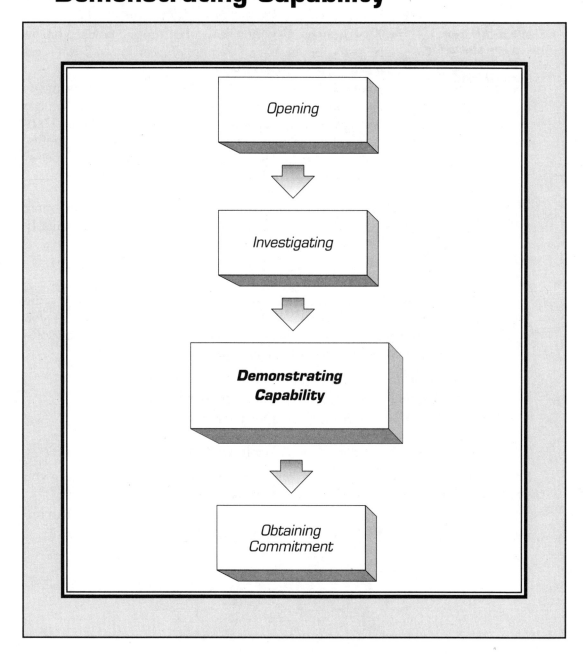

Overview

There are three ways to describe capabilities:

What different ways are there for describing capability?

- **Features**—Describe facts or characteristics of a product or service, e.g., *"We have forty skilled technicians ..."*
- **Advantages**—Describe how a Feature can be used or can help the buyer, e.g., *" Because of [that feature], you'd get quick response to a breakdown."*
- **Benefits**—Describe how a Feature or Advantage meets an Explicit Need expressed by the buyer, e.g., *"We can give you the one-hour response time you said you want."* Notice that we're using a very specific definition of Benefits. You may be familiar with the term but not the special way we're defining it here.

How do these different ways relate to sales?

Research shows that Benefits, as defined here, are the most persuasive way to describe solutions, and are particularly powerful in large or complex sales.

In large or complex sales, the result of using each of these methods is quite different from using them in a simple sale. For large or complex sales, you first have to develop the buyer's needs and build the value of your solution. Then, making Benefits will enable you to:

- Prevent objections, rather than having to "handle" objections.
- Help internal sponsors sell for you most effectively.
- Gain buyer support or approval for your solution.

To Demonstrate Capability effectively,

So what does that really mean?

- You need to complete the Investigating stage before you introduce your solution.
- Your buyer has to express an *Explicit Need* (not just an Implied Need) you can meet.

CHECK YOURSELF—DEMONSTRATING CAPABILITY

Before we go into more detail on Demonstrating Capability, check to see if you're clear about the differences between Features, Advantages, and Benefits by answering the following questions. Watch out for the strict way we define Benefits, so that a statement is only a Benefit if it meets an Explicit Need that the buyer has expressed.

	Feature, Advantage, or Benefit?
1. *The consolidated statement integrates a variety of information, so that you can reconcile all of your accounts at the same time.*	_____
2. *This course can accommodate up to 30 participants.*	_____
3. *The UV protection in the glass will extend the life of your instruments more than three years.*	_____
4. *Our leasing plan has an optional three-month trial period.*	_____
5. *By using the remote command capability, you can adjust the operating parameters whenever the demand curve deviates .01 above or below the baseline level.*	_____
6. *Ms. Crane, Sound to Go can satisfy the response time you said you needed during your busiest season, because we have fifty skilled technicians on call and also have a full inventory of all the latest equipment.*	_____
7. *Our system will reduce your current annual operating costs by 15 percent.*	_____
8. *Because our team has diverse and complementary skills, and expertise in your industry, we can provide a multifaceted approach to your particular problem.*	_____

Answers are on the next page.

1. Advantage The statement shows how the Feature (a consolidated statement) can help the buyer. Since the buyer has not expressed a need to reconcile all accounts at the same time, this is not a Benefit.

2. Feature The statement provides facts about the course.

3. Advantage The statement describes how the Feature (UV protection) can help the buyer. It's not a Benefit because no need has been expressed.

4. Feature The seller is describing a characteristic of the leasing system.

5. Advantage The statement describes how a Feature (remote command capability) is used.

6. Benefit The seller shows how the service can meet an Explicit Need (for quick response time) expressed by the buyer.

7. Advantage Since the buyer has not expressed a need to save money, it is not a Benefit. Even if the seller is sure that the buyer really needs to save money, it is only a Benefit if the *buyer* actually stated the need.

8. Advantage The seller is showing the buyer how the seller's service could help the buyer, but the buyer hasn't expressed a need for "a multifaceted approach."

Note: Don't worry if you found some of these examples difficult, especially the differences between Advantages and Benefits. Many people do, including experienced sellers. The good news is that the rest of this chapter will clarify and explain the importance of these distinctions.

Features, Advantages, and Benefits

Throughout this book, we've highlighted the importance of developing your buyer's needs by asking Problem and Implication Questions before introducing your solution. We've also shown you how to use Need-payoff Questions to build the buyer's desire for a solution. Now that you're ready to actually demonstrate the capability of your solution, what's the best way to do it?

The three classic ways of demonstrating capability are by using Features, Advantages, and Benefits. But each has quite different impacts—depending on whether the sale is large or small and where in the sales cycle they are introduced. In this chapter, we'll focus on the effects of Features, Advantages, and Benefits in large or complex sales, and how to use each most effectively.

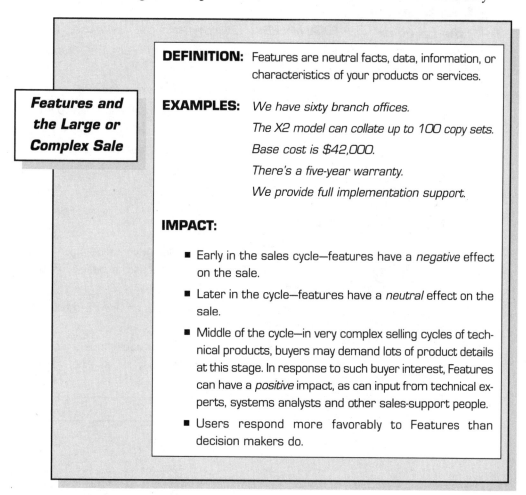

Features and the Large or Complex Sale

DEFINITION: Features are neutral facts, data, information, or characteristics of your products or services.

EXAMPLES: *We have sixty branch offices.*

The X2 model can collate up to 100 copy sets.

Base cost is $42,000.

There's a five-year warranty.

We provide full implementation support.

IMPACT:

- Early in the sales cycle—features have a *negative* effect on the sale.

- Later in the cycle—features have a *neutral* effect on the sale.

- Middle of the cycle—in very complex selling cycles of technical products, buyers may demand lots of product details at this stage. In response to such buyer interest, Features can have a *positive* impact, as can input from technical experts, systems analysts and other sales-support people.

- Users respond more favorably to Features than decision makers do.

Advantages

Advantages are what most sales-oriented books and training programs mean when they talk about "benefits." As *SPIN® Selling* explains, we first dubbed these "Type A Benefits" after testing a number of different definitions. During subsequent research in actual sales calls, we noticed that their effect on buyers is dramatically different from the effects of "Type B Benefits," or what we've since called "Benefits."

> ### Advantages and the Large or Complex Sale
>
> **DEFINITION:** Advantages show how products, services, or their Features can be used or can help the buyer.
>
> **EXAMPLES:** *... which means it's easy to use.*
>
> *And because of the duradyne rotor it operates silently.*
>
> *... so it provides extra security.*
>
> *Our international staff can meet your overseas needs.*
>
> *... which is the fastest available.*
>
> *Because of its efficiency, you'll save energy costs.*
>
> **IMPACT:**
>
> - Early in the sales cycle—Advantages have a slightly positive effect on call success, especially in the first visit.
> - Later in the cycle—Advantages are no more effective than Features.
> - Middle of the cycle—Advantages have a continuously less positive effect on buyers as the sales cycle proceeds.

Defining Benefits

We've seen that Features are fairly easy to define. But what about Benefits? People often define "benefits" in different ways. We've said that most sales training focuses on Advantages rather than on Benefits. Some people say benefits must show a competitive superiority, others emphasize that benefits must show a cost saving, while still others insist that benefits have to include a personal element ("you appeal") for the individual buyer, not just the buyer's organization.

We chose the very strict definition that "a Benefit meets an Explicit Need expressed by the buyer" because research shows that this definition, out of six we tested, is the one most clearly related to success in large sales.

We won't repeat here the process we went through to come to our conclusions, well described in *SPIN® Selling*. But it is essential to understand the distinctions between Advantages and Benefits as we define them, so that you can use Benefits to increase your impact on buyers.

True Benefits

Why do we insist that a statement can only be a Benefit if it meets an Explicit Need expressed by the buyer? Because if you make statements of this type, your calls are more likely to result in Orders or Advances. What makes these statements so much more powerful than other ways to describe your products or services? Two things:

1. **By linking your offering to the buyer's *expressed* needs, you demonstrate that you can help with the issues that matter most to your buyer.** Before you can give a Benefit, your buyer must first express a need. Your products or services, as we've seen, meet needs. It's not enough for you to assume that your buyer must have a need. By getting the buyer to express that need, you confirm its importance.

2. **Based on the definitions we've explained here, average sellers tend to use Advantages, which address only Implied Needs, while the most successful use Benefits, which directly respond to Explicit Needs.** The most successful salespeople first develop Implied Needs into Explicit Needs (clear wants or desires), using Implication and Need-payoff Questions. Then, once they have obtained Explicit Needs, they offer solutions *showing how they can meet those wants or desires.* Remember, average sellers offer solutions as soon as they have uncovered a problem—in other words, they offer solutions to Implied Needs.

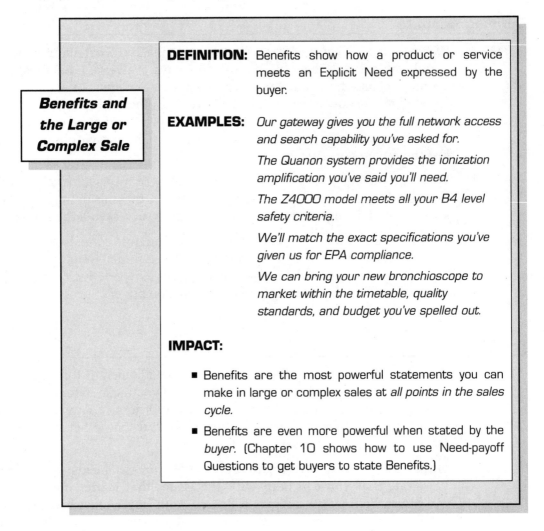

Benefits and the Large or Complex Sale

DEFINITION: Benefits show how a product or service meets an Explicit Need expressed by the buyer.

EXAMPLES: *Our gateway gives you the full network access and search capability you've asked for.*

The Quanon system provides the ionization amplification you've said you'll need.

The Z4000 model meets all your B4 level safety criteria.

We'll match the exact specifications you've given us for EPA compliance.

We can bring your new bronchioscope to market within the timetable, quality standards, and budget you've spelled out.

IMPACT:

- Benefits are the most powerful statements you can make in large or complex sales at *all points in the sales cycle.*

- Benefits are even more powerful when stated by the *buyer.* (Chapter 10 shows how to use Need-payoff Questions to get buyers to state Benefits.)

How Features, Advantages, and Benefits Affect Buyers

Features, Advantages, and Benefits each have a different effect on a buyer. For example, if a Jupiter car salesperson in Vermont reels off an array of features such as engine characteristics, electronics, climate control functions, and cosmetic options, what immediately fills the prospective buyer's mind? Yes, skyrocketing dollar signs:

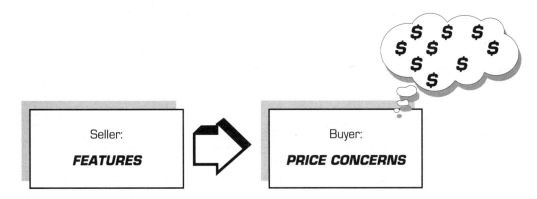

In the buyer's mind, each feature must add to the cost. So, by extension, the more Features recited by the seller, the higher the total price tag expected by the buyer.

Next, the same car salesperson tells that buyer how helpful it will be to have the four-wheel drive model with a built-in ski rack during the winter, which will provide both safety and convenience. But not having asked about the buyer's needs, how would the salesperson know that the buyer is planning to move to Florida in August? Will the buyer be impressed with the four-wheel drive option? Not on your life. S/he's most likely to *object* (if not leave the showroom).

Why? Because the salesperson is offering a solution where no Explicit Need has been expressed. When the buyer doesn't perceive a need for the capability being offered, the natural response is an objection.

In our final scene at the Jupiter showroom, the salesperson takes the time to ask Problem and Implication Questions. In doing so, the seller learns that the buyer makes long drives at night and suffers from eyestrain and lower back problems from the uncomfortable seat and driver position in the existing car.

Next, the salesperson asks Need-payoff questions, which build the value of finding a solution (a seat with lumbar support and extra bright headlights). As a result, the buyer expresses Explicit Needs—i.e., describing exactly what s/he'd want to include in a new car.

As the conversation continues, the salesperson identifies specific Benefits—showing how a new Jupiter with orthopedically designed seats will provide the lumbar support the buyer needs on long drives, while the high-intensity halogen headlights will prevent eyestrain. Because these are things the buyer wants, the seller doesn't get objections. Giving Benefits, the research shows, is the most effective way to demonstrate capability. The result:

Preventing Objections vs. Handling Objections

Let's look closer at the issue of Advantages leading buyers to respond with objections. We've seen that this occurs when the seller proposes a solution before building needs sufficiently. As a result, the buyer doesn't feel the problem is serious or urgent enough to justify an expensive solution.

That brings us back to the value equation presented in Chapter 6. To obtain the buyer's commitment to a sale, you need to build the value of the problems or needs enough to outweigh the cost of the solution. The value equation also shows that building the value of the buyer's problems actually *prevents* objections. Preventing objections ultimately costs sellers less than handling objections—less time, energy, and hassle. (For detailed case studies, see *SPIN® Selling*, pages 124–135.)

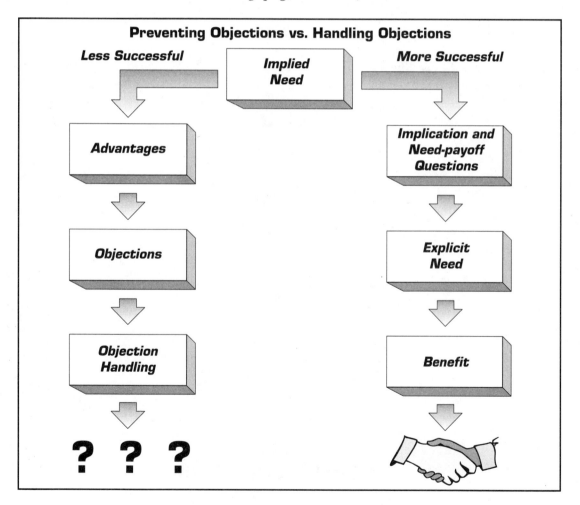

Handling Value Objections

Value objections emerge when the buyer raises doubts about the *value, worth,* or *usefulness* of the solution. In other words, to the buyer, the problem just doesn't warrant the costs (price, effort, time, hassle) of the solution.

Value objections, particularly those involving price, are the hardest for most salespeople to handle. Less successful sellers try to justify the cost of their products or services. The top salespeople we studied used a different strategy. They asked Implication Questions to build the seriousness of the buyer's problem, thereby increasing the value of their solutions.

The first step in planning Implication Questions to overcome value objections is to think of reasons why the problem is serious enough to justify an expensive solution.

Example

Problem the Buyer Should Take Seriously but Doesn't

Our present system is unreliable but we can live with it.

Price Objection to Your Solution

It's not worth the cost of changing it.

Unreliability:

Adds to cost.

May lose business.

Delays irritate customers.

Hurts our business image.

Increases operator frustration.

Reasons Why the Problem IS Very Serious

Now, try handling a value objection with one of your own buyers, the way our example showed you …

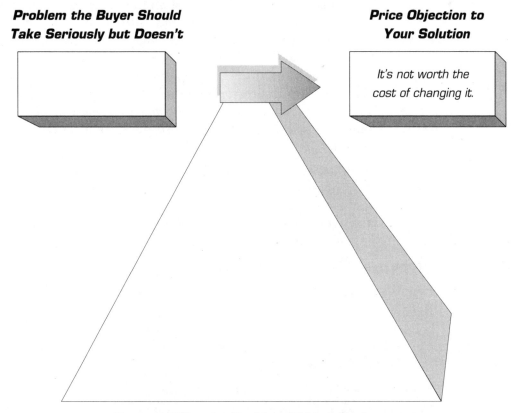

**Problem the Buyer Should
Take Seriously but Doesn't**

**Price Objection to
Your Solution**

*It's not worth the
cost of changing it.*

Reasons Why the Problem IS Very Serious

Tipping the Value Equation toward a Buy Decision

Did you notice that the "reasons" you came up with are also *implications*? Asking Implication Questions increases the seriousness or *value* of the problem side of the value equation. Asking Need-payoff Questions then builds the value of your solution. Together these components get buyers to express Explicit Needs.

Benefits Meet Explicit Needs

In summary, to state a Benefit under our definition, you have to:

- Show how you meet an Explicit Need, not an Implied Need. So a statement such as, *"You've got a problem with order entry; I can offer a program to solve that problem for you"* would *not* be a Benefit, because it addresses an Implied Need, not an Explicit Need.
- Meet an Explicit Need that has been *expressed* by the buyer. You can't make a Benefit based on assumed rather than stated need. So saying, for example, *"I imagine you'd want to save money and here's how we can do it for you ..."* would *not* make a Benefit because the customer has not expressed the need.

In large and complex sales, Benefits are the most effective statements you can make to buyers about your products or services. We've already seen that success in these sales depends on how well needs are developed. In offering a Benefit, you bring the needs development process to completion by showing how you can meet those needs.

What else makes Benefits so powerful in large and complex sales?

✔ **Benefits are more memorable than Features or Advantages.**

Buyers don't remember the Features or Advantages of your products or services. But they do remember their own Explicit Needs. Since Benefits are linked to those Explicit Needs, buyers will remember them long after Features and Advantages are forgotten.

✔ **Benefits have high impact on buyers throughout the sale.**

Features have a low to negative impact through the entire sale, and Advantages lose impact as the sale progresses. Only Benefits retain high impact throughout.

✔ **Benefits help your internal sponsors sell.**

In Chapter 10 you saw Need-payoff Questions used to rehearse internal sponsors. How did they accomplish that? The seller engaged the sponsor in identifying *payoffs,* which are another form of Benefits, so long as they show how the solution meets an Explicit Need expressed by that buyer.

Stating Benefits

Here's an exercise to practice stating Benefits. For our example the buyer is a hospital administrator and the salesperson sells paging systems. The seller starts by developing the buyer's problem, using Implication Questions to build the seriousness of the problem. The seller next asks Need-payoff Questions to get the buyer to state an Explicit Need. Then the seller states Benefits, showing how the product meets the Explicit Need.

Example:

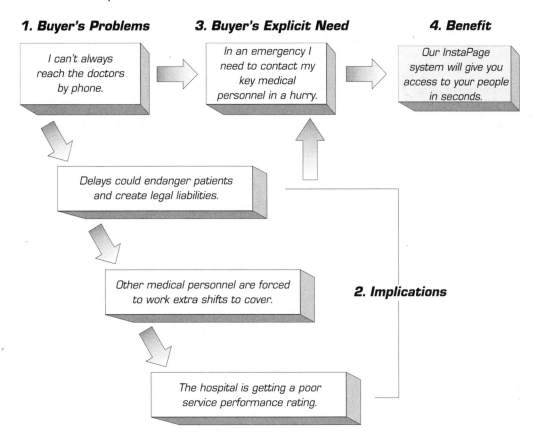

1. Buyer's Problems

I can't always reach the doctors by phone.

Delays could endanger patients and create legal liabilities.

Other medical personnel are forced to work extra shifts to cover.

The hospital is getting a poor service performance rating.

2. Implications

3. Buyer's Explicit Need

In an emergency I need to contact my key medical personnel in a hurry.

4. Benefit

Our InstaPage system will give you access to your people in seconds.

Now you try it, using an example of your own.

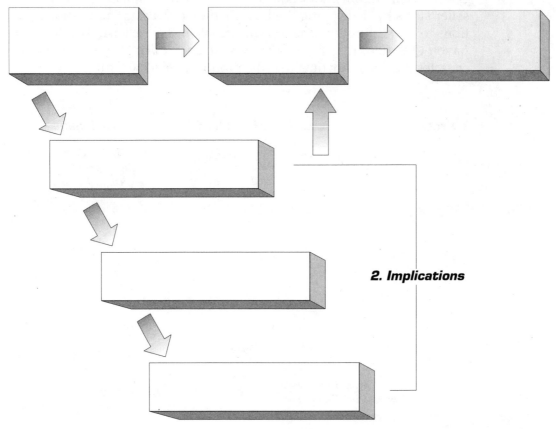

1. Your Buyer's Problems   **3. Buyer's Explicit Needs**   **4. Benefits You Can Make**

2. Implications

Beyond the Basics—Demonstrating Capability

More on Handling Objections

Preventing objections is always preferable to handling objections. Some interesting findings have emerged from our research:

✔ Objections are *not* buying signals—sellers who receive more objections do not experience more sales success.

✔ A majority of objections are created by the *seller.*

✔ Many objections occur because the seller offers solutions *too soon.*

Even when you use the SPIN® questions and develop buyer needs, some objections will occur. So it's essential to have objection-handling skills. But be careful not to get trapped into giving objection handling more prominence than objection prevention.

Why do objections occur? Often they occur because of factors beyond your control, such as buyer doubt, resistance to change, competition, inherently small buyer needs, or needs you can't meet with your product or service. For example, your buyer needs double-sided copying and your copiers don't provide that.

Objections fall into two overall categories:

1. **Value Objections**—where the buyer raises doubts about the *value, worth,* or *usefulness* of the solution you're selling, e.g., *"That's not much use to me," "It's too expensive," "I don't need it."*

   (You've already worked with value objections in this chapter. Use Implication and Need-payoff Questions to develop the buyer's need and to build the desire for a solution. The key is to move the buyer's need from Implied to Explicit.)

2. **Capability Objections**—where the buyer sees the value of solving the problem but raises doubts about the *capability, capacity,* or *genuineness* of the seller, the seller's organization, or the product or service being sold, e.g., *"I don't think you understand our business," "I'm sure it's not as easy as you claim."*

   There are two kinds of capability objections. Each requires a different strategy:

   Capability/Can't Objections—These kinds of objections occur when you don't have a capability to meet a need that is of high value to the prospect.

   Capability/Can Objections—These objections occur when you do have a capability but the buyer doesn't perceive that you have it.

Strategies for Handling Capability/
Can't Objections

The strategy for handling Capability/Can't Objections has two steps:

1. Acknowledge that you can't meet the need.
2. Increase the value of the capability you do have. Reemphasize the importance of the needs you can meet by using Need-payoff Questions and Benefit statements.

The aim of this strategy is movement. However, since you can't increase the buyer's perception of your capability, you have to increase the value of other needs for which you do have the capability.

Example

The seller, a senior manager in an accounting firm, is meeting with Jack Beck, president of a trucking company:

BUYER *Believe me, I understand your timetable, but I need to move faster than that.*

SELLER *Hmmm … Well, as you know, I don't think we can have that finalized in much less time than we talked about. But let's step back and see where we are.* [Acknowledges that he doesn't have the particular capability.]

BUYER *Well … okay.*

SELLER *Jack, I can see how moving that ahead a week or two would help. But I guess you have to consider the trade-offs—because you also said personalized service was important, and agreed that we're best able to provide it.*

BUYER *Yeah … You're right about the personalized service, but I'm concerned because getting a head start on next year's work could turn out to be crucial.*

SELLER *Yes, I understand … but could your need for personalized service prove to be important next year? For example, you've mentioned that you're planning an analysis of your cash management system. Isn't that a case where our help would be extremely important?* [Increases the value of the capability you do have.]

BUYER *True … we will need a lot of special help on that one.*

SELLER *So, the personalized service we've talked about might be important in a number of areas?* [Increases the value of the capability you do have.]

BUYER *No question … In fact, as we talk, more things are coming to mind. Let's see if there is some way we can look at this and try to….*

Here the seller is able to emphasize the importance of the existing capability (personalized service) by asking Need-payoff Questions, which helps the buyer to see its value.

Strategies for Handling Capability/Can Objections

There are three steps in the strategy for handling Capability/Can Objections:

1. Acknowledge the legitimacy of the buyer's concern. Show the buyer that you understand it's a reasonable concern.

2. Demonstrate your capability. Explain how you can provide the capability.

3. Show proof, where necessary. Provide a source(s) of proof that genuinely supports that you are able to meet the need.

Example

The seller is a bank officer meeting with the buyer, who is president of a small company that is about to enter the international market.

BUYER *Regarding the foreign exchange area, it seems to me I'd be better off going with one of the money center banks.*

SELLER *Uh-huh.*

BUYER *Since the money center banks do have experience in that area, I suspect that they'll be able to provide us with better foreign exchange rates.*

SELLER *Well, you certainly do want the best rates* [acknowledges the legitimacy of the objection], *but today you don't have to be a money center to be competitive in the foreign exchange market.*

BUYER *Oh ... Why's that?*

SELLER *Well, it's a matter of having the right kind of information service. We're in direct contact with the European market. So we're always aware of the best prevailing rates.* [Demonstrates capability of the seller's organization.]

BUYER *Well, I think I understand that, but this is our first marketing effort in Europe, and we do need to get off on the right foot.*

SELLER *Uh-huh. Well, what I think we should do is have you talk with Bob Townsend at Borax. He just addressed this same issue. I'll also send you a publication just put out by* The Wall Street Journal, *which I think will be of some help.* [Shows proof by offering other supporting sources.]

BUYER *Okay ... Sounds good.*

Capability/Can Objections are handled most effectively by using a simple straightforward strategy. The major error that occurs in handling this kind of objection is failing to acknowledge the legitimacy of the buyer's concern.

Launching New Products or Services

One area of Demonstrating Capability that even the most experienced salespeople handle poorly is the introduction of new products or services.

We've studied many product and service launches and found that, when an offering is new, salespeople give three times as many Features and Advantages than they do when selling existing offerings. And their level of questioning falls off dramatically. Because they're not asking questions, they tend to introduce new product solutions very early in the discussion, which, as we've seen, is not an effective way to sell.

Even worse, their enthusiasm for the new offering can make them product-centered instead of buyer-centered. As a result, they talk about the bells and whistles of the new product or service, instead of asking about the buyer's needs. Then it becomes all too easy, especially if you were introduced to the product or service in terms of its Features and Advantages, to communicate about it with your buyers in the same way. Don't let it happen to you!

The best strategy for launching new products or services consists of a consolidation of steps you practiced in Chapters 5, 8, and 9:

New Product/Service Launch Strategy

1. Identify the problems your new product or service can solve, or the needs it can meet for buyers.
2. List the kinds of buyers who might have these problems or needs.
3. Identify specific accounts where these problems or needs could exist.
4. Develop the Problem and Implication Questions you can ask to probe for those problems.
5. Keep your focus on the buyer's actual needs and problems when you have your face-to-face meeting. In that way you can show the Benefits of your new product or service, and avoid the trap of selling on Features and Advantages.

DEMONSTRATING CAPABILITY—SUMMARY CHECK

1. Which of the following are true statements? **True?**

   a. Benefits are the most effective way to demonstrate capability.

   b. It's best to present lots of Features at the start of a sale.

   c. The impact of Advantages diminishes as the sale progresses.

   d. Objections are the most likely response to Advantages.

2. Which of the following statements by the seller are Benefits? **Benefit?**

   a. *I assume you want to save money and our service will do that for you.*

   b. *You said you want changes in this department. Our productivity improvement program would certainly change things.*

   c. *You've said you need good sound quality, which the noise-reduction facility on this system provides.*

   d. *This software package will be a big benefit to you.*

   Feature?
   Advantage?
   Benefit?

3. Which of the following is a Feature, an Advantage, a Benefit? **(F, A, B)**

   a. *The entire assembly measures only 10×3×6 inches.*

   b. *An overhead value analysis has to be carried out at all levels to be effective.*

   c. *So you're rapidly running out of office space, Mr. Albert. I have just the thing for you. Our newest desktop copier does two-sided copying, which will cut your filing space requirements in half.*

   d. *And another thing about taking this vacation in May: It means you can avoid the summer tourist crowd.*

   e. *We offer a bulk-purchase plan and, because of it, we can offer you a bigger discount.*

Answers are on the next page.

1. **(a), (c), and (d) are true.** Giving Features at the beginning of a sale is at best neutral, often raises price concerns, and can actually jeopardize the sale.

2. **Only (c) is a Benefit.**

   (a) is not a Benefit because the need is assumed rather than expressed.

   (b) is not a Benefit because the need for change is too broad and general to be linked to telephones. The need is not Explicit.

   (c) is a Benefit because the seller links the product (a noise reduction facility) to an expressed and Explicit Need of the buyer.

   (d) is definitely not a Benefit, even though some sellers try to convince buyers with statements like this.

3. **None of these statements is a Benefit.**

   (a) is a Feature. Despite the tempting word *only*, the seller is simply giving data about the product.

   (b) is a Feature. The seller is describing a characteristic of overhead value analysis.

   (c) is an Advantage. This is a very difficult example. It may seem at first glance to be a Benefit, but the buyer's need is only Implied, not Explicit. Although the buyer raised a problem about lack of space, the seller's quick link to double-sided copying is unlikely to have a positive effect on the buyer, who may find it irrelevant. Statements like this should thus be treated as Advantages. It *would* be a Benefit if the buyer had first developed the need using a Need-payoff Question such as, *"So would you find it useful to have a way to reduce your filing space?"*

   (d) is an Advantage. The Feature is May and the Advantage is avoiding crowds.

   (e) is an Advantage. The Advantage of the bulk-purchase plan is the discount. Because no Explicit Need was expressed, there is no Benefit.

12

Sharpening Your Skills

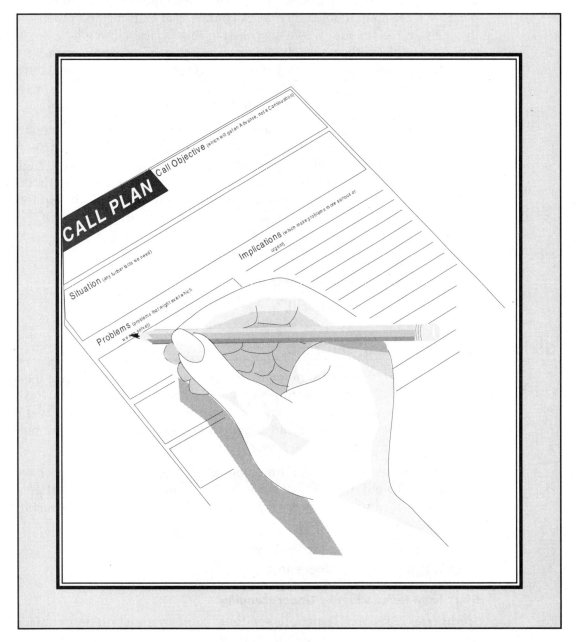

Within the illustration:

CALL PLAN

Call Objective (which will get an Advance, not a Continuation)

Implications (which make problems more serious or urgent)

Situation (any further facts we need)

Problems (problems that might exist which we can solve))

What to Expect

What bottom-line improvement should you expect from developing your SPIN® skills? The first thousand people we trained in these skills averaged a 17 percent increase in their sales results. Will that happen for you? Many people have more than doubled their sales volume after learning and practicing the skills and techniques we've described in this *Fieldbook*. But a little application of simple mathematics should warn you that, based on an average increase of 17 percent, if some have more than doubled their sales, there must also be some who were below average or who didn't benefit at all. How do you make sure that you're in the group that gets above-average results?

The bad news is that there's no magic formula to give you a cast-iron guarantee of better sales results. But the good news is that we have strong evidence showing that, if you get just three things right, there's a very high probability that you will achieve superior results from these methods. None of these three things is particularly difficult, though each requires hard work, persistence, or a shift in perspective. They are:

- **Get on the buyer's side of the table.**
- **Invest in planning.**
- **Give yourself a periodic checkup.**

Let's look at each one in detail.

Get on the Buyer's Side of the Table

One of the hardest shifts for many traditional salespeople is to change their thinking so that they stop acting like a seller and, instead, see the world from the buyer's perspective. When we talk about getting on the buyer's side of the table, we don't mean trying to manipulate the buyer by pretending to see things from the buyer's point of view.

What we are talking about is a fundamental shift in perspective. You have to abandon the old mentality of seller vs. buyer. In its place you must genuinely share the buyer's concerns. Specifically, it means that you must shift your thinking in two respects:

- **Shift from persuading to understanding.**
- **Shift from a product focus to a buyer focus.**

Shift from Persuading to Understanding

Traditionally, most salespeople see their primary function as persuading. This leads them to argue the merits of their products, and to become advocates for their companies and for the services they offer. What's wrong with persuasion or advocacy? Simply, it's not the perspective that the world's most successful salespeople take.

From working with many hundreds of top salespeople in fields as diverse as consulting and chemicals, we find that the primary perspective of top salespeople is *understanding* rather than persuading. They see their first and foremost responsibility as understanding the world from the buyer's point of view. This perspective has a dramatic impact on how they sell. Because they really care about what their buyers think, they ask more questions than traditional salespeople. They are less inclined to talk prematurely about products and solutions. And, because they are sincerely trying to understand their buyers' issues, this communicates to their buyers and they are seen as genuine.

What does this have to do with improving your SPIN® skills? A whole lot. If you set out to understand, then you are more likely to ask questions, less likely to give Features and Advantages and less likely to jump in too soon with solutions. Also, research suggests that you'll listen better and be more likely to hear the buyer's real needs.

A nice illustration of how true this is in practice comes from one of the world's largest telecommunications companies. Their sales force was asked to go to a sample of their existing customers and conduct a survey to understand what these customers were doing, how their environment was changing, and what issues they were facing. The consultants who had designed the survey emphasized that, in order to provide objective data, the sales force should just try to understand these customers better and on no account should use the survey calls to sell.

In the three months that followed, to the combined amazement of the consultants, the company's management, and the sales force, there was a 35 percent increase in sales to the customers involved in the survey compared with all other customers. The reason was simple. Because the survey forced the sales force to really focus on understanding their customers, they uncovered new needs and saw additional productive opportunities. Even better, customers responded very positively to being understood and invited salespeople back to do more business.

So take a tip from top salespeople. An easy way to improve both your skills and your sales is to see each call as an opportunity to understand rather than to persuade.

Shift from a Product Focus to a Buyer Focus

One metaphor for the role of salespeople is that they are a bridge between products and customers. The seller is the connector, the link that brings buyers and products together. The effective salesperson has to understand both ends of this bridge—to understand on the one side buyers and their needs and on the other side the capabilities of products and services. Which end of this bridge is more important for sales success? The evidence seems to show that:

- Most salespeople are more comfortable and proficient at understanding their products than at understanding their buyers.
- Very successful salespeople have adequate product knowledge, but superior knowledge of customers.
- Salespeople with the highest product knowledge don't make the most sales.
- If forced to make a choice, buyers are more likely to deal with those who best understand their needs than with those who best understand products or services.

So, if you are a typical salesperson, there's a good chance that right now you are putting too much emphasis on the products and services side of the bridge. Shifting your attention to understanding buyers will probably pay off for you in terms of results.

That means things like:

- Keeping up with business and industry trends that affect your buyers.
- Reading current business journals rather than product manuals.
- Having a real curiosity about what's going on inside the buyer's organization and asking lots of questions about changes that have an impact on the buyer's operation.

A relentless interest in the buyer's business issues has paid off for those who have behaved this way. We once did a study for IBM to find why some salespeople learned how to sell much more quickly than others. We found that on the whole those with the greatest knowledge of computers had only average learning curves.

The fastest learners—who became the future high fliers of IBM—were the ones whose focus on their buyers made them curious about business issues. Even without training, these fast learners naturally asked SPIN® questions because they were really interested in their buyers' problems and the implications behind these problems. In consequence, every call that they made gave them an opportunity to learn through their questions about business issues, industry trends, and areas of importance to customers.

In contrast, those with the highest product knowledge were more likely to spend time in calls talking about IBM and its capabilities. They learned much less about their buyers and their results were poorer as a consequence. So one way to improve both your selling and your SPIN® skills is to be sure you shift from a product focus to a buyer focus.

Invest in Planning

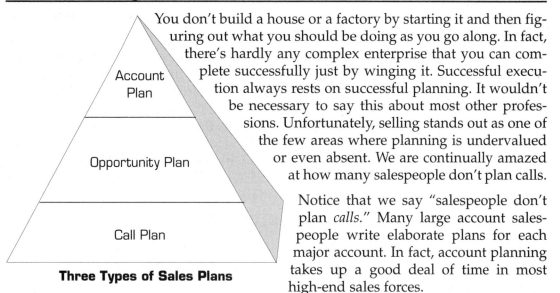

You don't build a house or a factory by starting it and then figuring out what you should be doing as you go along. In fact, there's hardly any complex enterprise that you can complete successfully just by winging it. Successful execution always rests on successful planning. It wouldn't be necessary to say this about most other professions. Unfortunately, selling stands out as one of the few areas where planning is undervalued or even absent. We are continually amazed at how many salespeople don't plan calls.

Notice that we say "salespeople don't plan *calls.*" Many large account salespeople write elaborate plans for each major account. In fact, account planning takes up a good deal of time in most high-end sales forces.

Three Types of Sales Plans

But, to succeed in achieving your major account plan you must successfully execute a number of *opportunities.* We define an *opportunity* as a series of sales calls that could culminate in a major sale. Much less time is spent planning opportunities than planning accounts. Yet, unless the component opportunities succeed, the account plan will fail.

Plan Your Calls

But let's move down one level of detail. Each opportunity is made up of a number of calls and each call must be successful for the opportunity to be met. So individual sales calls are the building blocks out of which opportunities are constructed, and a series of opportunities must be achieved in order to successfully execute an account plan. Our concern is that few salespeople pay enough attention to planning the humble sales calls that are the fundamental units making up account success.

If there was just one piece of advice we could give people to improve their selling, it would be this: *Plan your calls.* Worry less about grand strategy and more about the tactics of each call. Think of an actual sales call you are planning to make in the near future. How clear are you about the objective of the call? Do you know exactly what outcome you hope to achieve? What specific questions do you plan to ask? What planning tools are you using to help you to prepare? If you don't have good answers to these questions, you probably don't have an adequate call plan. Call planning is the bedrock on which sales strategy is built.

Time and time again in our work we've seen elegant account strategies fail because the call execution skills just weren't there. We're not saying that strategy is unimportant. Our book, *Major Account Sales Strategy* (McGraw-Hill, 1989), gives clear evidence that overall account strategy is crucial to success in major accounts. The problem that we've seen over the years is that no strategy is better than the capacity to execute it and—on an individual call level—execution more often than not lets the strategy down. So what advice would we give you to help your call planning? Three points:

1. First, plan Advances.
2. Then plan what to *ask,* not what to tell.
3. Use a planning tool to help you prepare.

Take a call you'll be making in the near future and try this advice out for yourself.

1. First, Plan Advances

In Chapter 4 we talked about call outcomes and the importance of Advances. We explained the distinction between Advances and Continuations.

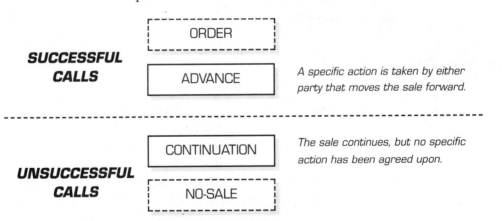

SUCCESSFUL CALLS

ORDER

ADVANCE

A specific action is taken by either party that moves the sale forward.

UNSUCCESSFUL CALLS

CONTINUATION

The sale continues, but no specific action has been agreed upon.

NO-SALE

Simple though this distinction is, it's vitally important to successful planning and, even more important, it's vital to successful selling. One of the differences between top salespeople and their less successful colleagues is that top performers are very clear about the Advances that are possible from each call and they set call objectives based on the highest realistic Advance they can achieve.

Let's try this out with a call you intend to make.

- First brainstorm at least *five* possible Advances you could make from the call.
- Check that each Advance you have listed is an action that is realistic and that really moves the sale forward.
- Choose the best of these Advances as your *Call Objective*. The best Advance is the one that most moves the sale forward while being realistic and achievable.

Finally, choose a *fallback objective*—a less ambitious Advance that still moves the sale forward but will be easier to achieve if your first Advance proves unobtainable.

Example

Call: *New material call on Jeff Love, Buyer at Metco*

ADVANCE: [a specific action that moves the sale forward]	Moves sale forward?	Easy to achieve?	First choice and fallback
Set up a meeting with buyer's V.-P. Manufacturing.	*A lot*	Very hard *until we have data to present.*	
Get their technical people to review studies on new material.	*A little*	Easy. *This is their normal procedure.*	*Fallback*
Persuade buyer to visit Ohio test site.	*A little*	Hard. *Buyers rarely visit sites.*	
Get their technical unit to do laboratory evaluation of the new materials.	*Moderate*	Moderate. *Lab owes us one for providing purity checks last year.*	*First choice*
We take their spec and work up a prototype sample.	*A lot*	Very Hard. *Would cost us $40K and Fred would go crazy.*	

Now try planning Advances for your own call:

Call: _____

ADVANCE: [a specific action that moves the sale forward]	Moves sale forward?	Easy to achieve?	First choice and fallback

One of the characteristics of very successful salespeople is their ability to think of a wide range of ingenious Advances. Less successful salespeople often find it difficult to think beyond the most obvious ways to move the sale forward. Use this exercise to stretch your thinking and to generate as wide a range of Advances as possible. We've asked here for five, but if you can think of ten, so much the better.

2. Plan What to Ask, Not What to Tell

Once you've selected your first choice Advance and your fallback, what do you do next? You plan the call itself. It's here that we sometimes play a nasty little trick on salespeople we're working with. Before we discuss planning, and without any warning, we ask them to take a piece of paper and jot down a quick plan for a sales call they intend to make within the next week.

We then ask them the all-important question: *"Did you plan what you were going to **tell** or what you were going to **ask**?"* Almost 80 percent of our victims have planned what they are going to tell. The 20 percent who have planned what they intend to ask are generally the most experienced and successful members of the group.

If you'd been in one of these groups, what would you have done? Be honest: Would you really have been in the 20 percent who planned questions?

If, like most people, you plan what you intend to tell, then no wonder it's hard to ask effective questions while you're selling. Remember:

- Plan it, or you just won't do it.
- If you want to get on the buyer's side of the table, you must shift from persuading to understanding. Asking questions is the best way to understand your buyer.

The secret to asking effective questions lies in planning them. One way to do this is just to write down a list of questions. That's how many successful salespeople plan. However, an even better way is to use a planning tool.

3. Use a Planning Tool

CALL PLAN   **Call Objective** (which will get an Advance, not a Continuation)

Get client to schedule a joint pre-proposal planning meeting to review their criteria.

Situation (any further facts we need)
- *Identify current staff's expertise/capabilities.*
- *Find out about staff changes during last 12 months.*
- *Find out about any budget constraints.*

Problems (problems that might exist and that we can solve)	**Implications** (that make problems more serious or urgent)
Technical challenges	*cost of O/T could impact profit margins*
	lack of expertise could affect quality
	delay in project completion could give
	market advantage to the competition
Pressures on existing staff	*could lead to staff turnover*
	hiring new in-house staff would add to
	costs and extend learning curve
	staff could defect to competition
Other projects being neglected	*client's reputation could suffer*

Explicit Needs (we hope to develop)	**Benefits** (we can then offer)
- *Project to be on time, with high quality and within budget* - *Keep existing staff up to date and happy* - *Other projects to get done, too*	- *Our technical expertise can fill their gap cost-effectively* - *Can support and train existing staff* - *Allows key staff to work on other projects*

CALL PLAN

Call Objective *(which will get an Advance, not a Continuation)*

Situation *(any further facts we need)*

Problems *(problems that might exist and that we can solve)*

Implications *(that make problems more serious or urgent)*

Explicit Needs *(we hope to develop)*

Benefits *(we can then offer)*

How to Use the SPIN® Call Plan Form

The SPIN® Call Plan form is a simple and intuitive way to plan sales calls. We've evolved and tested it with thousands of salespeople. There are copies at the end of the book for you to use in planning other calls. Here are some points to help you get the most from it.

1. **Advances**

   It's hard to plan good questions if you don't know where you want the call to go. So always start by planning an Advance that moves the sale forward. Remember that you usually have a choice of Advances. Choose the one that gives you the best combination of forward movement with ease of achievement. The more ambitious your Advance is in terms of forward movement, the more important it is to also plan a fallback objective for the call in case your first Advance proves unachievable.

2. **Situation Questions**

   Plan only *essential* Situation Questions that give you information you can't find from other sources. We advise people to plan Situation Questions last. That way they put most of their energy into planning more powerful questions. It's easy to come up with a long list of Situation Questions that you would like to ask, but doing so won't help you sell. The skill of planning Situation Questions lies in reducing your list. Ask yourself whether a Situation Question you would like to ask is really essential. If not, particularly if you are selling to a senior executive, it's better to leave it out.

3. **Problem Questions**

   Plan to uncover at least three problems that you can solve with your products or services. By planning a variety of problems, you'll have the flexibility to move to a new problem area if the one you first explore turns out to be unproductive. You'll find it easier to plan Problem Questions if you start by identifying the problem areas you intend to explore and only think of the questions after you have chosen the areas. So, for example, you might first decide that this buyer has problems in the areas of reliability and speed. Once you've chosen these areas, you might plan questions such as, *"Do you find your present system too slow?"* or *"How many failures are you getting?"*

4. Implication Questions

These are the hardest questions to plan but the ones where planning has the greatest rewards. A single good Implication Question can make the sale. As with Problem Questions, you should identify implication *areas* first and then frame your Implication Questions. You don't need many Implication Questions to create impact. A couple of good questions for each problem area will usually be enough.

5. Explicit Needs and Benefits

Remember that a Benefit always meets an Explicit Need. So when you plan the Benefits you hope to offer, each one first depends on developing an Explicit Need. It's good discipline to plan Explicit Needs and Benefits together because, without Explicit Needs, there will be no Benefits.

Get into the habit of using a call planning tool like this one. Remember that you can't have an effective sales strategy without good calls. Planning is worth the effort. There's no other single thing you can do to improve your selling that compares with systematic call planning. Make it a way of life and see how your results improve.

Give Yourself a Periodic Checkup

We are all creatures of habit. Even if we have the right skills, even if we know the correct way, bad habits creep in. We get lazy; we take shortcuts. Imperceptibly, without ever reaching conscious awareness, we develop habit patterns that hurt our selling. Let me give you a personal example.

When I first discovered the SPIN® model, I realized that I needed to improve my own selling. I was doing too much telling. I was jumping in with solutions too quickly. Most of my questions were Situation Questions. In short, the discoverer of the SPIN® model was lousy at selling. But I was determined to change and to take my own medicine. Through lots of practice and through careful planning of my sales calls I slowly improved until—though I say so myself—I was pretty good at it. Even better, my results improved dramatically and I brought in some big orders for Huthwaite, my consulting firm. I thought I was all set for a dynamite career in sales.

Then, with the success of *SPIN® Selling,* I had the misfortune to become well known.

I was invited to make speeches all over the world, including such exotic places as Cleveland, Ohio. I was on the guru circuit. I talked, I spoke, I expounded. In other words, I was doing a lot of telling and not much seeking. But—and here's the point of the story—I didn't realize that bad habits were creeping up on me. In my own mind I was still the same old lovable SPIN® seller who had questioned his way to success.

One day a client asked me to participate in a television documentary about the SPIN® model. They wanted to film me making a sales call to serve as an example for their salespeople. I agreed and so we set up a call and arrived at the buyer's office complete with video crew. Afterwards, as I watched the tapes, I realized that what I had intended as a shining example was actually a dreadful warning. I counted the questions I had asked. There was a total of seven—and six of them were low-powered Situation Questions. To my horror, I saw that in the months on the guru circuit I had returned to some of my bad habits. I was *telling* my way through the SPIN® model. Instead of asking Problem Questions, I was telling the buyer about problems. I was explaining implications, not asking about them. It was a disgraceful exhibition and I was thoroughly ashamed of myself.

Since then, I've given myself a checkup from time to time to keep myself honest. I advise you to do the same. I take a small tape recorder into the call with me. With the buyer's permission, I tape the call and analyze it afterwards. These checkups help me see when I'm slipping back into bad habits. They also highlight areas where I need to improve and they help sharpen my skills. I've learned a lot from analyzing my own selling.

The next page shows the tool I use to help myself.

This example is from one of my own checkup calls. I asked the buyer if I could tape record the call. Don't be nervous about doing this. Hundreds of salespeople I've worked with use the SPIN® checkup tool. They regularly ask buyers for permission to tape calls. They rarely get refusals and, in many cases, buyers have expressed admiration for the professionalism of people who care enough to work at improving their skills.

Example

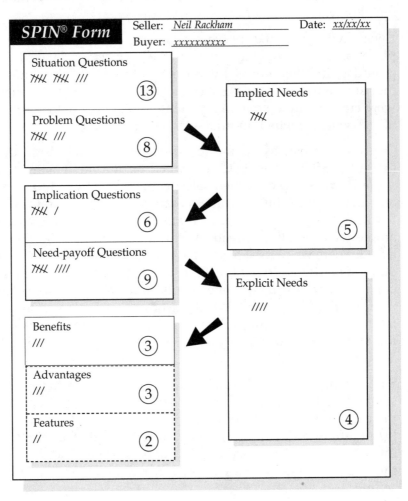

When I got home, before I played the tape, I reread my SPIN® Call Plan to help remind me of what I was trying to achieve in the call and what questions I had planned to ask. I then played the tape once all the way through without stopping. I asked myself these questions:

- Did the call go as I had planned? In particular, did I achieve the Advance I had hoped for?
- Was there anything that went well, that I might want to remember for future calls?
- Was there anything less effective than I would have liked?

Assessing the Call

Here are my actual notes on the answers to these questions:

Did the call go as planned?

Succeeded in getting the planned Advance [an invitation to present a partnering proposal to the General Managers at the Paris meeting] but the client's lack of interest in follow-up to the Two-Tier Program surprised me. Perhaps I should have tried for a more aggressive Advance like a European pilot.

What went well?

Useful discussion on the market segment model. I must remember to use the "fuel the engine" example in Paris. Good development of implications around the problem of consequences of ineffective executive selling to global accounts.

What wasn't effective?

Didn't listen well to Jeff's concern about reduction of sales costs. On tape he said it three times and I didn't pick up on it. I still don't listen when I get enthusiastic.

As you can see, I had a few surprises. You'll probably find, as I did, that you hear things on the tape that you missed entirely during the call itself. And, with luck, you'll find some things worth remembering for future calls.

Finally, I replayed the tape, using the SPIN® Form to analyze my questions. Every time I asked a question, I made a tick mark in the appropriate box. That way I could see the number of questions I asked in the call and how they were distributed across the SPIN® categories. Since I've done this a lot, I was able to play the tape without stopping while I analyzed the behaviors used in the call. If you haven't done this before, stop the tape after each behavior while you decide which type of question you asked, or whether you were describing a Feature, an Advantage, or a Benefit.

On the next page you'll find a blank SPIN® Form for analyzing one of your calls. You'll find an additional copy at the end of the book.

Analyze One of Your Own Calls

Use this SPIN® Form to analyze a recording of a call you've made. If you don't have an opportunity to record a real call, role play a call with a friend to give you material for this analysis.

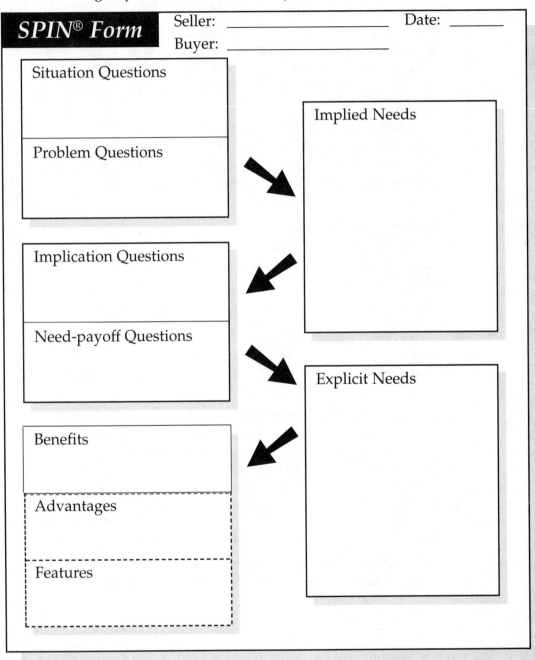

SPIN® Form

Seller: _____ Date: _____

Buyer: _____

Situation Questions

Problem Questions

Implication Questions

Need-payoff Questions

Benefits

Advantages

Features

Implied Needs

Explicit Needs

Interpreting Your SPIN® Checkup

What do the numbers from a SPIN® Form mean? In my case, for example, I asked 13 Situation Questions. Is that too few or too many? I asked six Implication Questions. Is that good or bad? The answer is that the precise number matters much less than the overall pattern. I asked more Situation Questions than any other type, but that's normal. The overall pattern is a good one. I asked about problems [eight Problem Questions] and developed some of those problems with the six Implication Questions and nine Need-payoff Questions I asked.

Where would I like to improve? Two areas could be better. This was a complex call and I think I could usefully have asked even more Implication Questions. Another area that could be improved is Benefits. I gave three Benefits but, listening to the tape, I heard an opportunity for at least one more that I missed.

To help you interpret your own pattern, here are four typical SPIN® profiles:

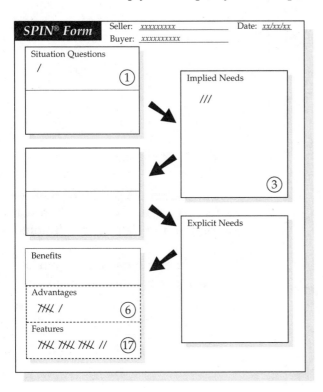

Profile 1: Eddie Expert

This is a typical profile of an over-zealous expert. Very few questions—in this case just one. Lots of Features—telling more about the product than the buyer could possibly want to know.

Improvement: Ask questions—*any* questions.

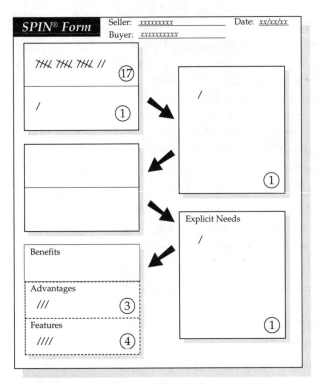

Profile 2: Just the Facts, Ma'am

This profile is typical of the inexperienced person who feels safe asking for facts. Unfortunately it's boring to the buyer.

Improvement: Work on planning and asking more Problem Questions, particularly by using the SPIN® Call Plan.

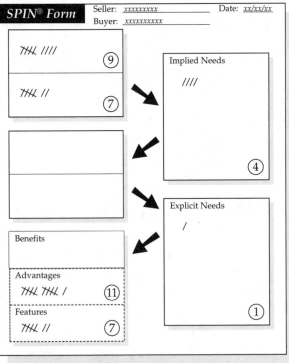

Profile 3: Go for the Jugular

This is the classic profile of the experienced person who can't resist jumping in too soon with solutions.

Improvement: Hold back from offering answers. Instead, plan and use Implication Questions.

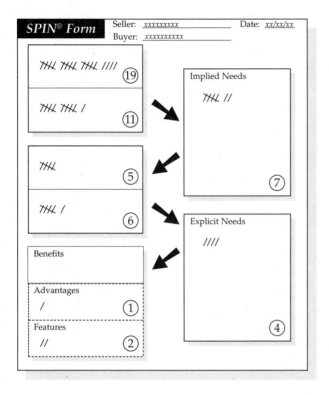

Profile 4: Solution-Short

It's a rarer profile, but sometimes we see sellers like this one who know how to sell but aren't comfortable talking about their products. They ask good questions, but don't know the Features, Advantages, and Benefits of their offering.

Improvement: Work on product knowledge.

Your own pattern may not look exactly like any of these profiles. However, by analyzing your selling in this way, you'll gain new insights into how well you use questions and you'll see opportunities to improve your selling.

In this chapter we've offered advice and tools for sharpening your selling skills. We've suggested that you:

- **Get on the buyer's side of the table,** by shifting from persuading to understanding and by shifting from a product or service focus to a buyer focus.
- **Invest in planning,** using a tool such as the SPIN® Call Plan.
- **Give yourself a periodic checkup,** by recording your calls and analyzing them afterwards.

This approach—and using the Call Plan form and the SPIN® Form—has been field tested by thousands of salespeople. It works. It takes time and effort but, if you could talk with the many people who have used this approach, they would tell you that their investment was worthwhile.

13
Getting Help and Helping Others

Once I was staying with friends in Bombay who took me to a village wedding. Among the musicians was a teenager with a violin. I was struck by two things about him. First, he played the complex *raga* scales with a fluid elegance that was awesome. The second striking thing was that he didn't put the violin under his chin as Western musicians are taught to do. He held it upright, like a small cello resting on his knee. I asked if this was the local style of playing and learned that it wasn't. This young man had inherited the violin from an uncle and, by trial and error, learned how to play it. He never had a single music lesson and, until very recently, had never seen or heard any other violin player, which was why he held the instrument in such a peculiar way. It was a tribute to his determination and ingenuity that he played so well. I couldn't help thinking, if only he'd had some help from a good teacher, he could easily have been a world-class virtuoso.

Since that day, I've come to realize just how unusual that young man was. Very few people are able to develop complex skills alone and unaided. Whether we're talking about music, art, sports, or selling, most of us need some outside assistance if we hope to improve. We need a teacher, a guide, or a coach. A fieldbook like this can certainly be a help. It can, for example, show you the selling equivalent of how to hold the violin under your chin. But it's no substitute for another person who can coach you—who can show you the finer points of violin playing. There *are* a few natural geniuses in this world like the young violinist who can find their own way unassisted. However, most of us need support from another person if we intend to polish and perfect our skills.

Where can you get help? Large organizations usually have some organized way to help their people develop and refine selling skills. They offer training programs or they have experienced sales managers whose job is to coach and guide salespeople. But if you work for a smaller company, you are rarely so lucky. Small organizations usually lack the resources to offer top class training. Their managers are often snowed under with a dozen priorities that leave them with little or no time for helping people develop selling skills. Even worse, if you are selling alone, if you are your company's only salesperson or you are a one-person organization, then there's no source of help inside your organization. Over the years, I've received many hundreds of calls from people looking for help. They want to go beyond the things that a book can teach, but they haven't an experienced sales manager or access to a good company training program. What can they do?

Here's the answer I give. First, be sure you've learned all you can reasonably get from teaching yourself. If you're using a book like this one, set about the kind of systematic planning, practice, and self-analysis that we described in the last chapter. Even without additional help, it's possible to go a long way if you are prepared to put effort into the exercise material. Next, think about three sources of help. These are:

- Coaching from a mentor.
- Two-way coaching.
- Help from outside organizations.

Let's examine each option more closely.

Coaching from a Mentor

Your manager, or a more experienced salesperson, may be willing to give you some time to help you develop skills. If you're lucky enough to have this source of help available to you, use it well. Here are three ways in which an experienced mentor can be invaluable for developing skills.

- **Call Planning**

  Every minute spent in planning to make a call go right is worth ten spent in reviewing a lost sale or a call that went wrong. Use your mentor to help coach you in planning. And do plan a *specific* call. That's a much better use of time than planning overall strategy. Too often we see salespeople go for help to experienced managers or colleagues, then spend their mentor's scarce time on discussing only the big picture or the overall strategy. But the sad fact is this: No strategy is better than your capacity to execute it. The lowly sales call is a far better place to start improving your skill than flying at 30,000 feet over an account. Use your mentor to help you think about a specific call, about what needs to uncover and what questions to ask.

- **Role Playing**

  If you have access to a skilled mentor, then there are few better ways to learn than through role playing. After you've planned together, role play the call asking your mentor to play the buyer role. If possible, tape record the role play. Then replay the tape asking your mentor to comment. If you get to a section of the tape that you think you handled badly, or where you were unsure what to do, then ask your mentor to role play a suggested alternative way to handle the problem.

- **Real Calls**

  Best of all, if your mentor has time available, go on a call together. Choose a call that's not too difficult, such as one involving an existing buyer where the discussion will be relatively easy and routine. Remember that your mentor is there as a coach. That means that *you must do the selling.* You'll learn a lot less if your mentor sells for you. The role of the coach is to observe your selling and to give you feedback afterwards.

Two-Way Coaching

Many people don't have access to an experienced coach or manager. So they feel doomed to learn alone. However, one of the most exciting and interesting ways to improve skills doesn't need a mentor who has more experience than you possess. It's called *two-way coaching* and it's a method that allows you to learn from others who are also working to improve their selling. The basic idea is simple. Team up with another person who also wants to improve their skills. It doesn't even have to be someone in your own company, as this example illustrates.

Two-Way Coaching in Action

George S. was a partner in a small accounting firm. He was given the job of clientele development [aka "selling"]. George was not entirely comfortable in this new role because he hadn't previously done any selling. Nevertheless, he read a few sales books and decided to give it a try. He soon found that very few of his meetings with potential clients were turning into business. Unsure what to do, he talked to a friend of his during a local Chamber of Commerce meeting. This friend was an attorney in a partnership that specialized in real estate and property law. As it happens, the lawyer was just about to take on a similar business development role for his partnership. So they decided to help each other. They met every Friday evening and worked together to plan a call that each intended to make during the following week. They set call objectives and listed questions they intended to ask. Looking back on it, George told us, "We weren't very sophisticated about how we planned, but planning together turned out to be a big help." They also reviewed earlier calls at their regular Friday meeting. Sometimes they would ask the client if they could tape record calls. They played the tapes over together and each learned a lot. When George told us about their experiences, he said, "At the start, we were two bright but inexperienced professionals. But, by combining resources, we learned quickly. I got further in a couple of months with two-way coaching than I'd done in the whole year when I'd been selling solo."

Here are the steps to go through if you want to try two-way coaching.

1. **Choose a partner.**

   As we've seen, it doesn't have to be someone more experienced than you are, or even someone from the same company or the same type of business. The crucial thing is that you both would like to improve your selling and you are both prepared to put effort into helping each other.

2. **Agree on a learning contract.**

   Set out clear principles for how you and your partner will two-way coach. Our suggested rules would be these:

   - *Tell it straight.* We'll learn best from straight feedback. So we won't pretend things were effective if they weren't. We'll tell it as it is, not say things to boost each other's egos. Mutual admiration societies don't build skills.

   - *Place facts before interpretations.* When we listen together to a tape of a call, or a tape we've made of ourselves role playing, we'll always begin by discussing the objective facts, such as, *"You asked three Problem Questions in that section"* before we go on to interpretations such as, *"I didn't think that was a very good question to ask."*

   - *Keep it confidential.* We're going to learn things about each other and our skills. We'll keep this between us and not discuss the content of our two-way coaching discussions with others.

3. **Plan together.**

   When you get together, plan two calls, one call each that you'll be making before your next meeting. Plan the Advance and the questions you intend to ask. Use the Call Plan from this *Fieldbook* as your basic planning guide and discussion document. Explain to each other why a particular question would help uncover or develop needs and give each other suggestions for additional questions.

4. **Record the call.**

   Most buyers are very receptive to having the call recorded, especially if you explain that you planned it with a colleague who can't be at the meeting but who was interested in hearing what happened.

5. **Review it together.**

   Use the SPIN® Form from the last chapter to analyze and discuss the call. Remember that it's facts first and interpretations second.

6. **Keep it up.**

You won't learn much from doing it just once. The plan–do–review cycle must be repeated several times before it starts to work. Most people who have tried two-way coaching say that you should give it four or five meetings before you see real results.

Two-way coaching [or Peer Coaching as it's sometimes called] holds great potential. We think that it's an exciting way to set about improving skills. If you decide to look for coaching help, either from a mentor or from two-way coaching, you might find it useful to read the chapter on sales coaching in our book *Managing Major Sales* (Rackham and Ruff, Harper Collins, 1991).

Help from Outside Organizations

A final option is to look for help from consultants or training organizations who run sales training programs. I say "final option" because I've generally thought of this as a last resort. Many of the programs offered to the public at large by the thousands of sales training vendors are low-level and ineffective. It's hard to sort out which ones offer real value and which are a waste of time and money. How can you make sure that training or seminars offered by outside organizations will really help your selling? Here are a few hints to help you.

- **Beware of extravagant claims.**

  Any program that suggests it can "double your sales," let you "close every deal," or "have buyers eating out of your hand" is likely to be pure snake oil. The responsible vendors are the ones who make modest claims.

- **Beware of "new and dramatic breakthrough" programs.**

  Every few months we come across claims that someone has found a dramatic new approach to selling. Invariably, when we look closely, we have been disappointed. The only dramatic thing about most of these programs is their marketing hype.

- **Beware of "as used by IBM and other (rich and famous) companies" claims.**

  While I was working for Xerox, we trained more than three thousand of their salespeople and, in the process, got to know their training very well. So we were surprised to see, in a sales magazine, a program we'd never even heard of advertising itself as "the sales training that Xerox uses." Xerox trainers were also puzzled. So they checked it out. They found that the "as used by" claim was based on the fact that two people from a branch of Xerox had been on the program. Like most large companies Xerox sent a participant to every new seminar just to check out whether there was anything interesting. I wonder how many people responded to the advertisement thinking that they were getting something widely used and endorsed by Xerox.

Caveat emptor. There are excellent training vendors out there who can really help you. But don't be taken in by the claims of those who are more interested in your money than your needs. Check references carefully. Look at track records. Ask to talk with satisfied users, and, if possible, to a company that has put more than 100 people through the program. In that way you can tell that someone thought the program worthwhile enough to put several groups through it.

Of course, we too are in the training business and would love to help you. (After all, who knows the SPIN® model better than we do?) But, whether you get help from this *Fieldbook* alone, from coaching with other people, or from outside sources like ourselves, the important thing is that *you* work to improve your selling. Effective selling is the proverbial long journey that starts with a single step. It's our hope that our research and this book have helped you a mile or two along the road to success.

SPIN® Forms

SPIN® Form Seller: _____ Date: _____

Buyer: _____

Situation Questions

Problem Questions

Implication Questions

Need-payoff Questions

Benefits

Advantages

Features

Implied Needs

Explicit Needs

CALL PLAN

Call Objective *(which will get an Advance, not a Continuation)*

Situation *(any further facts we need)*

Problems *(problems that might exist and that we can solve)*

Implications *(that make problems more serious or urgent)*

Explicit Needs *(we hope to develop)*

Benefits *(we can then offer)*

CALL PLAN

Call Objective *(which will get an Advance, not a Continuation)*

Situation *(any further facts we need)*

Problems *(problems that might exist and that we can solve)*

Implications *(that make problems more serious or urgent)*

Explicit Needs *(we hope to develop)*

Benefits *(we can then offer)*

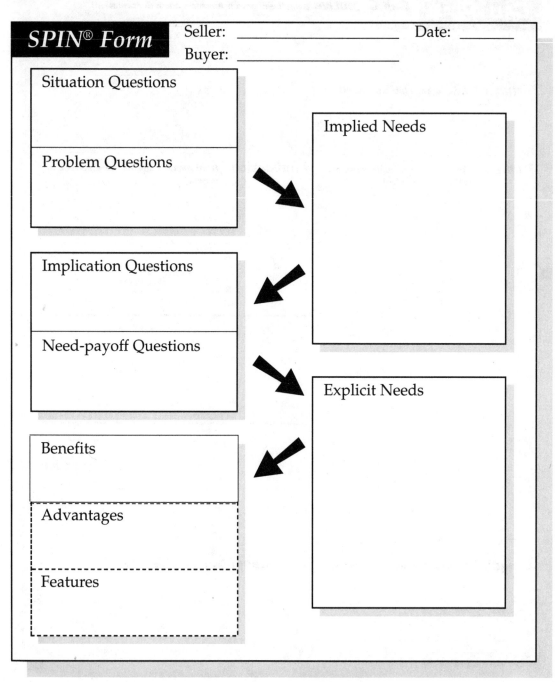

SPIN® Form   Seller: _____   Date: _____
                  Buyer: _____

Situation Questions

Problem Questions

Implication Questions

Need-payoff Questions

Benefits

Advantages

Features

Implied Needs

Explicit Needs

SPIN® Form

Seller: _____   Date: _____

Buyer: _____

Situation Questions

Problem Questions

Implied Needs

Implication Questions

Need-payoff Questions

Explicit Needs

Benefits

Advantages

Features

WORKSHEET—PROBLEMS SOLVED BY YOUR PRODUCT/SERVICE

Product or Service: _____   Customer: _____

Characteristic of Product/Service	Problem This Solves for the Buyer

WORKSHEET—WORKING BACKWARD TO THE PROBLEM

Explicit Need	Implied Needs
Your Solution That Is Superior to the Competition's	**Problems This Could Solve**

Explicit Need	Implied Needs
Your Solution That Is Superior to the Competition's	**Problems This Could Solve**

GETTING HELP FROM HUTHWAITE

Huthwaite, Inc. is an organization focused on helping companies improve sales productivity. Our work is derived from extensive research and analysis, and is based on the notion that successful selling should be nonadversarial, customer-centered, and needs-driven.

We offer a variety of training programs, workshops, seminars, and consulting services to help organizations assess and improve sales effectiveness.

We would welcome hearing from you about your own selling successes, concerns, and needs. Write or call and let us know what's working for your company, where you'd like to see/get improvement, and how we might help you.

For further reading, *Major Account Sales Strategy* (Neil Rackham, McGraw-Hill, 1989) offers powerful strategies for selling to major accounts, based on the entire buyer decision process, and provides models and tools to take sales effectiveness to the next level.

Huthwaite, Inc.
Wheatland Manor
15164 Berlin Turnpike
Purcellville, VA 22132
United States

(540) 882-3212

Index

About the Author

Neil Rackham is the founder and president of Huthwaite, Inc., a leading sales consulting, training, and research firm. His book *SPIN® Selling* has sold more than 150,000 copies. Mr. Rackham is recognized as a pioneer in sales force effectiveness and success, and is widely credited with bringing research and analytical methods to the field of sales force improvement.

Refer questions to:

Huthwaite, Inc.
Wheatland Manor
15164 Berlin Turnpike
Purcellville, VA 20132
U.S.A.
Tel: (540) 882-3212
Fax: (540) 882-9004